A Taste of the West Country

A collection of original recipes created by
Taste of the West award-winning chefs and producers

wemakemagazines

A catalogue record for this book is available
from the British Library.

ISBN 978-0-9933352-1-1

Published by We Make Magazines Ltd
wemakemagazines.co.uk

Editor: Jennie Cooper
Sub-editor: Clare Hunt
Designer: Jeff Cooper

Thanks to Belinda Berwick and Emma Grainger
and the rest of the team at Taste of the West; also
to Jody Spencer.

Contents

Martin's Meats Longhorn beef sirloin, mushroom
ketchup, wild garlic and asparagus   20

The Artisan Kitchen's Blaisdon Red Plum Jam soufflé
with plum ripple ice cream   24

Golden-fried hen's egg, chive hollandaise
and asparagus on a potato cake, using
Blackdown Hills West Country Eggs   30

Roasted breast of Hinton Harvest Sasso chicken,
braised leg ravioli, crispy wing, spring vegetables
and tarragon   38

Smoked salmon, asparagus and Godminster Brie
with Cracked Black Pepper tart   44

Chorizo, wild garlic and Godminster Brie with
Cracked Black Pepper croquettes and lemon aioli   46

Lemon pots with raspberry sauce and meringue,
using Rebecca's Kitchen Lemon Curd   52

Dorset Lobster mac and cheese
with Palmers Best Bitter sauce   56

Chesil Smokery smoked duck salad with blackberry ketchup   62

Sea bass with sizzled ginger, chilli and spring
onions, served with Watercress Company Baby Leaf Salad   66

Mediterranean Sharpham Ticklemore Goat cheese slice   72

Gazpacho soup with Favis of Salcombe crab   76

Favis of Salcombe crab benedict with blanched asparagus   82

South Devon Chilli Farm chocolate fondant   86

Sharpham Cremet and Jerusalem artichoke risotto   90

Coronation brown shrimp with spiced pineapple chutney, using Otter Vale Coronation Sauce 94

Roasted breast of duck, charred chicory with fig and date jus, using Otter Vale jelly and relish 96

Dressed native blue lobster cocktail using Bell & Loxton Rapeseed Oil for the mayonnaise with fennel, apple & chilli 100

Smoked ham hock & Quicke's Mature Cheddar terrine with Jail Ale pickled onion, cheese toasty and cheese beignet 106

Orange Elephant Banoffee baked alaska 112

Scallops with Kittows Hogs' Pudding 118

Twice-baked Cornish Yarg soufflé 122

Roast Cornish rabbit with Boddington's Berries
Blackberry Conserve and fresh blackberries   128

Spice-crusted Cornish Duck Company duck breast
with polenta, plum sauce, Savoy cabbage and squash balls   132

Gluten-free Polgoon Sparkling Elderflower Wine
and raspberry sponge   138

Wheal Charlotte Pizza, using Cornish Yarg   144

Scallops served with Boscastle Farm
Shop Hogs' Pudding   148

Foreword

Farm shops, pop-up cafés, street food, artisan bakers, delis and producers, chefs and restaurants – you'd struggle to find anywhere else in the country with as rich a food and drink scene as here in the West Country. Speak to the farmer and he is as passionate as the butcher about his produce, who is as exacting in preparing his cut of meat as the chef is who cooks it for you. We have a lot to celebrate.

So our second recipe book, *A Taste of the West Country,* has once again coupled together award-winning chefs and producers from Taste of the West to create this sought-after keep-sake. Each pair comes from across Gloucestershire, Somerset, Dorset, Devon and Cornwall, bringing you fresh, honest and seasonal recipes.

Using ingredients readily found around the region, these dishes have been created specifically for this book – so prepare to impress your friends and family. You needn't be an accomplished cook to enjoy trying these recipes either, all have been compiled with simplicity (and maximum flavour) in mind.

There is no better way to celebrate a true Taste of the West Country, while supporting the local food and drink industry. We hope you enjoy cooking our recipes.

John Sheaves
Chief Executive, Taste of the West

All recipes serve 4

Gloucestershire

Martin's Meats Longhorn beef sirloin, mushroom ketchup, wild garlic and asparagus

Recipe by Robert Cox, Head Chef, Tudor Farmhouse Hotel, Clearwell

Ingredients

800g piece of beef sirloin
8 asparagus spears
50g toasted hazelnuts, roughly
    chopped
20 small girolle mushrooms
400g salted butter
20g beef dripping
5 sprigs thyme
2 cloves garlic
8 kohlrabi leaves
8 turnip leaves
4 nasturtium leaves
12 wild garlic flowers

For the wild garlic purée

100g baby spinach
300g wild garlic leaves
50g salted butter
50g double cream

For the mushroom ketchup

500g chestnut mushrooms
6g salt
20ml sherry vinegar
30ml dark soy sauce
20g caster sugar
4g agar agar

To make the wild garlic purée

1   Melt the butter in a large pan and add the spinach and the garlic leaves. Sweat until fully cooked. You can check this by rubbing the leaves between your fingers – if it totally disintegrates it's cooked.
2   Place the sweated leaves into a blender with the double cream and blend on full power for around two to three minutes until totally smooth. Season.
3   Push the purée through a fine sieve and then cool down as quickly as possible.
4   Just before you are ready to cook the beef, warm the purée in a pan, check the seasoning, put it into a squeezy bottle and keep warm.

To make the mushroom ketchup (in advance)

1   Finely chop the mushrooms then mix with the salt and hang in a muslin cloth over a bowl overnight to drain. Reserve the liquid but discard the mushroom pulp.
2   Bring the soy, sugar and sherry vinegar to the boil and then use the mixture to season the mushroom juice to your own taste.
3   Add the agar agar to the liquid, bring to the boil and whisk constantly for about 10 seconds until fully dissolved, pour into a tray and place in the fridge to set.
4   Once set, place in the blender and blend to a thick purée consistency, retain at room temperature.

Continued on page 22...

To make the beef and asparagus

1 Remove the beef from the fridge and allow to rest, uncovered, for at least two hours before cooking.
2 Peel the asparagus and trim off the woody ends.
3 Preheat a medium-sized frying pan to a medium heat then add in the beef dripping. Heavily season the beef with salt and pepper then put it into the pan, fat side down. Allow the fat to render out for around three to four minutes, then add 100g butter to the pan with the thyme and garlic. Colour the beef on all sides, turning every minute to ensure even cooking. Once coloured, turn the heat down to low and continue to cook as desired (for medium rare, as per the picture, the core temperature will be 45°C). Rest the meat in a warm place for as long as you cooked it, brushing with its butter every five minutes.
4 Bring 300g butter, 300ml water and 9g salt to the boil to make an emulsion. Add the asparagus then turn down to a low heat. Cook for five to eight minutes, then remove from the emulsion, place on a warm tray and coat in the hazelnuts. Keep the emulsion.

To serve

1 Trim both ends of the beef then cut into four evenly sized slices. Very lightly season the exposed pink meat with salt and place on warmed plates.
2 Place two spears of asparagus next to the beef then put a large dot of wild garlic purée just above it.
3 Cook the girolles, kohlrabi and turnip leaves in the emulsion for 30 seconds, then drain and scatter over the beef and asparagus.
4 Place a teaspoon of the mushroom ketchup on the plate and garnish with the garlic flowers and nasturtium leaves.

"Taste everything! The difference between a good meal and a great one is in the details; ensuring that everything is seasoned correctly will really elevate your cooking."

Robert Cox

The Artisan Kitchen's Blaisdon Red Plum Jam soufflé with plum ripple ice cream

Recipe by Robert Cox, Head Chef, Tudor Farmhouse Hotel, Clearwell

For the crème patissière
250ml milk
½ vanilla pod, scraped
40g caster sugar
4 egg yolks
15g plain flour
8g cornflour

For the plum ripple ice cream
600ml milk
400ml double cream
4 vanilla pods, scraped
10 egg yolks
40g glucose syrup
200g plum jam

For the soufflé
75g plum jam
75g crème patissière
200g egg white
50g caster sugar

4 buttered and sugared soufflé
   ramekins
Ice-cream machine

To make the crème patissière
1 Bring the milk and vanilla to the boil, then remove from the heat and cover with clingfilm to infuse for 30 minutes.
2 Whisk the egg yolks and sugar together, then beat in the flours. Pass the milk through a fine sieve, add 200ml to this mixture and whisk. Pour it back into the remaining milk, bring to the boil over a medium heat, whisking continuously until very thick.
3 Pass through a fine sieve (don't let it go cold) then cool with a layer of clingfilm on top to prevent a skin forming.

To make the ice cream
1 Bring the milk, cream and vanilla to the boil. Pour the mixture over the egg yolks, glucose and sugar and whisk. Pass through a fine sieve back into the pan and bring to 84°C to pasteurise. Cool.
2 Pour into an ice-cream machine and churn. Ripple the plum jam through the ice cream and freeze to set.

To make the soufflé
1 Place the jam and 75g of the crème patissière into a bowl and whisk.
2 In a separate bowl whisk the egg whites to soft peaks, add the sugar and whisk for a further 30 seconds.
3 Add the egg white to the jam mixture in three batches.
4 Spoon into the ramekins, leaving a flat surface flush with the top. Run your thumb around the lip of the ramekin

Continued on page 27...

to make a small indentation around the edge. This will ensure the soufflé rises without catching.

5 Bake at 190°C/gas mark 4 for around eight minutes until well risen.

6 Two minutes before the end of the cooking time, scoop the ice cream onto the plates so you can serve the soufflé as soon as it's ready.

Robert Cox, Head Chef, Tudor Farmhouse Hotel, Clearwell

"What grows together goes together! Many of the ingredients for the beef sirloin dish are either foraged from the surrounding area or picked from our kitchen garden. There is a balance of flavour in terms of salt, sweet, sour, bitter and umami with each ingredient contributing to the overall taste. The dish also has a lightness but intensity of flavour that I really associate with spring. Having the meat at room temperature and dry before cooking is essential. Drying it allows it to brown really well, meaning maximum flavour, and the temperature means the meat cooks more evenly and faster.

For the plum soufflé, preparation is critical, all elements of the dish must be ready before the soufflé can be cooked. Winging it is not an option!

My proudest kitchen moment was cooking for Raymond Blanc and him loving it! Legend."

Sarah Churchill, Owner & Producer, The Artisan Kitchen, Gloucester

"My company makes delicious, luxury high-fruit-content sweet preserves. We supply wholesale throughout the UK and internationally to over 400 speciality food stores, farm shops, delicatessens and food halls.

For myself, when sourcing ingredients, they have to be of the finest, freshest quality – the very best. The local heritage plums I use in my preserves are a fine example of the very best fruit. Sourced locally along the banks of the River Severn from a fifth-generation orchard grower, the fruit is handpicked from the trees and turned into delicious jam within hours of picking.

We have recently taken on an allotment, which is a great stress buster and just lovely to be out in the fresh air. The nicest way to unwind is walking our dog Scamps, especially on our foraging trips for lovely wild Gloucestershire fruits."

Somerset

Golden-fried hen's egg, chive hollandaise and asparagus on a potato cake, using Blackdown Hills West Country Eggs

Recipe by Rebecca Owen, Head Chef, The Lordleaze Hotel, Chard

For the potato cake

800g cold, mashed potato
1 red onion, diced
2 cloves of garlic, crushed
60g butter
3 tbsp olive oil
1 tbsp plain flour for dusting
Pinch of sea salt
Pinch of freshly ground black pepper

For the golden eggs

100g plain flour
6 eggs
200g Panko breadcrumbs
Vegetable oil, for deep frying
Splash of white-wine vinegar

For the asparagus

1kg asparagus spears
30g butter
Iced water

For the chive hollandaise

1 tbsp fresh lemon juice
2 free-range egg yolks
750g clarified butter, melted
Handful of chives, chopped
Water, as necessary

To prepare the eggs

1 Boil a medium-sized pan of water, add a splash of white-wine vinegar, stir the water to form a whirlpool, lower the temperature and soft poach four of the eggs for two minutes. Refresh in iced water.

2 Sprinkle the flour onto one plate, the breadcrumbs onto another, then beat the two remaining eggs in a bowl. One at a time, carefully dredge the soft poached eggs first in the flour, then dip them in the beaten eggs, then roll in the breadcrumb mixture until completely coated. Place each coated egg onto a sheet of greaseproof paper and chill in the fridge for at least one hour.

To prepare the potato cakes

1 Heat the butter and one tablespoon of the oil in a medium-sized frying pan until foaming.

2 Add the onion, reduce the heat to medium and cook whilst stirring for five minutes. Add the garlic and cook for a further minute. Allow to cool.

3 Combine the mashed potato, cooled onion and garlic mixture, salt and pepper and mould into four burger-shaped patties.

To cook the asparagus

Cook in boiling, salted water for two to three minutes. Drain well and refresh in iced water.

Continued on page 32...

To make the hollandaise sauce

1 Bring a third of a small pan of water to the boil, then reduce the heat until the water is simmering. Suspend a heatproof bowl over the pan without allowing the base of the bowl to touch the water.

2 Add the lemon juice and egg yolks to the bowl and and whisk continuously for four to five minutes, or until the mixture is pale and has doubled in volume.

3 Remove the egg and lemon mixture from the heat. Gradually add the clarified butter in a thin stream, whisking continuously, until all of the clarified butter is incorporated into the mixture. Add two tablespoons of water to the hollandaise sauce if necessary, to loosen. Mix in the chopped chives and keep warm until ready to use.

To serve

1 Shallow fry the potato cakes in the remaining two tablespoons of oil until crisp and golden on both sides. Keep warm.

2 Heat the oil in a deep-fat fryer to 190°C. Alternatively, heat the oil in a deep, heavy-based frying pan until a cube of bread sizzles and turns brown when dropped into it. Carefully lower the eggs into the hot oil and fry for three to four minutes, or until crisp and golden-brown. Remove from the pan using a slotted spoon and set aside to drain on kitchen paper.

3 Re-heat the asparagus in a medium hot pan, coating it with melted butter.

4 Place the potato cake on a plate, top with the asparagus and the golden egg. Drizzle the hollandaise sauce around the edge of the plate.

"Use English asparagus in season or substitute with fresh green seasonal vegetables such as spinach."

Rebecca Owen

"...it gives me extreme pleasure when I see a field full of happy hens out in the sunshine..."

Ken Cottey

Rebecca Owen, Head Chef, The Lordleaze Hotel, Chard

"This dish is inspired by texture! Crispy and crunchy with rich unctuous egg yolk it can't be beaten. The hollandaise sauce and the potato laced with garlic take it to another level. Everything is enhanced by garlic – it keeps the soul and the taste buds alive!

My top cooking tip for this dish is do it properly, don't cut corners, take a little more time and give it love and attention – it makes all the difference. The best way to poach eggs is to boil a pan of water and add a splash of white-wine vinegar. Crack the eggs into individual cups, stir the boiling water to create a whirlpool effect, lower the eggs into the water one by one (cooking two at a time) and reduce the temperature to a gentle poach. Cook for two minutes then remove and eat, or refresh in iced cold water for use as in this recipe."

Ken Cottey, Managing Director, Blackdown Hills West Country Eggs, Chard

"We are a family farm situated on one of the highest points on the Blackdown Hills in Somerset. Having produced fresh, free-range eggs for over 13 years, we now continue the process by packing them in our newly built packing centre and delivering them all over the country.

With our own 30,000 birds and some other like-minded producers in and around the West Country we supply some of the major supermarkets, as well as selling wholesale and to food service. But we haven't forgotten our roots and still have a van delivering to shops, pubs, etc in local towns.

The welfare of our birds is very important and it gives me extreme pleasure when I see a field full of happy hens out in the sunshine, pecking and scratching around. My wife says I spend more time with them than with her, which is true!"

Roasted breast of Hinton Harvest Sasso chicken, braised leg ravioli, crispy wing, spring vegetables and tarragon

Recipe by Olivier Certain, Head Chef, Clavelshay Barn Restaurant, North Petherton

Ingredients
1 Hinton Harvest Sasso chicken, legs, breasts and wings removed
2 extra chicken wings
2 extra chicken breasts
5 stems fresh tarragon
Seasonal spring vegetables
1 tbsp butter
1 tbsp breadcrumbs
1 tbsp plain flour
1 egg
Vegetable oil for deep frying

For the ravioli dough
250g pasta flour
2 medium eggs plus 3 yolks
Pinch of saffron powder

For the chicken stock
Carcass and skin from the chicken
1 carrot, peeled and roughly chopped
1 onion, peeled and quartered
1 stalk celery, roughly chopped
6 black peppercorns
1 dried bay leaf
3 fresh parsley stalks
1 sprig fresh thyme

To make the chicken stock
1 Preheat the oven to 180°C/gas mark 4. Roast the chicken carcass for an hour and a half, until brown, turning halfway through cooking.
2 Put the carcass into a pan with the remaining stock ingredients and cover with cold water. Bring to the boil, skim off any scum that forms, then place a lid on the pan and simmer very gently for two to three hours.
3 Strain the liquid into a large bowl and set aside to cool. Discard the bones and vegetables.

To cook the chicken
1 Brown the chicken legs with a splash of oil in a pan. Once browned, partly cover the legs with water, put a lid on the pan and braise over a low heat for four and a half hours. Once cooked, cool the legs, pick off the meat and chill.
2 Vacpack the breast with a sprig of tarragon and cook in a water bath for 45 minutes at 68°C. Once cooked, refresh in iced water. Alternatively, place the breasts into a pan of cold water, bring to the boil then reduce them to a simmer for around 10 minutes. Remove from the heat and allow the chicken to fully poach through as the water cools.
3 Place the wings into a pan, cover with water and bring up to the boil. Turn off the heat and set aside, allowing the wings to poach as the water cools.

Continued on page 40...

To make the ravioli

1 Whisk together the eggs, yolks and saffron. Place the flour in a food processor. With the motor running, gradually add the eggs until the mixture resembles breadcrumbs.

2 Tip the dough onto a work surface and knead for two to three minutes until smooth. Wrap in cling film and chill for a minimum of 30 minutes before use.

3 Once rested, roll the dough into thin sheets using a pasta machine. Transfer to a floured surface and using a 12cm, cutter cut out eight rounds.

4 Brush the edges of four rounds with egg wash and place a ball of the braised chicken leg meat in the middle of each. Put another round on top and press the edges together to seal, stretching the dough slightly and moulding it around the filling with your fingers to make sure there are no gaps. Neaten the edges with scissors then blanch the ravioli for four minutes before refreshing in cold water. Chill until ready to serve.

To serve

1 Make a simple sauce by bringing the chicken stock to the boil and allowing it to bubble vigorously until reduced by a third. Once reduced, keep warm.

2 Heat the oven to 180°C/gas mark 4. Add one tablespoon of butter to a roasting tray and heat in the oven until foaming. Add the poached chicken breasts, baste with the butter and roast for 15 minutes. Cover to keep warm and set aside to rest.

3 Remove the cold poached wings from the liquid and pat dry with kitchen paper. Dredge in flour, coat in lightly beaten egg then roll in breadcrumbs. Deep-fry in vegetable oil until crisp and golden.

4 Meanwhile, cook the ravioli for four minutes in simmering water. Drain.

5 On a plate, arrange a chicken breast along with a golden wing and a ravioli. Drizzle over the sauce and garnish with a sprig of tarragon. Serve with lightly cooked spring vegetables.

Top Tip: If you don't need the chicken stock immediately, chill it overnight, skim off any fat that has formed on the surface and use within three days.

> "The inspiration for my recipe came from meeting Dawn. She cares so passionately about her chicken that I wanted to produce a dish that really did it justice"
>
> Olivier Certain, Clavelshay Barn Restaurant

Dawn Quince, small-scale off-grid farmer, Hinton Harvest, Hinton St George, near Crewkerne

"I produce award-winning, free-range, orchard-reared chicken and guinea fowl as well as award-winning salad leaves. I supply Somerset including Bath and Bristol.

The best part of my job is looking after our land in a sustainable way. We bought a derelict tree nursery in 2009 and the neglect had turned it into a haven for wildlife. We share our field with badgers, rabbits, green woodpeckers, swallows, several thousand bank voles and numerous butterflies and moths! I'm really proud that I can provide a lovely orchard environment for my chickens and guinea fowl without impacting on all the other things that live here. We don't use any herbicides or pesticides, have a solar-powered bore-hole pump, a compost toilet and solar panels for electricity.

We have a 1959 International tractor called 'Ian' – he's needed fixing for ages and we can *never* get around to it. He only starts with the help of 'Easy Start'. If we added up all the money we'd spent on 'Easy Start' we could probably buy a new tractor!

I'm not very good at unwinding from work – there's always something to do or worry about. However, show me a barrel of local golden ale and I'll give unwinding my best shot!"

Smoked salmon, asparagus and Godminster Brie with Cracked Black Pepper tart

Ingredients

120g smoked salmon
200g fresh asparagus
100g Godminster Brie with Cracked
    Black Pepper, sliced
3 medium eggs
2 egg yolks
100ml double cream
150ml full-fat milk
Zest of a lemon
Salt to taste

For the pastry

200g unsalted butter, diced
400g plain flour
90ml cold water
1 egg, beaten
Pinch of salt

To make the pastry

1 In a food processor, mix together the butter, flour, salt and two-thirds of the water. Blitz for about 15 seconds. Check the consistency, if it's too dry and crumbly you may need to add the remaining water. Blitz for a further five seconds.

2 Lightly flour a work surface and gently knead the pastry until it comes together. Flatten into a disk, wrap in cling film and place into the fridge for at least 30 minutes.

3 Preheat a baking sheet in the oven to 220°C/gas mark 7. Roll out the pastry on a lightly floured surface to line a greased 23cm loose-bottomed tart tin. Trim and discard any excess pastry. Prick the base all over with a fork, line with baking parchment and fill with baking beans. Return to the fridge for 10 minutes.

4 Blind bake the pastry case for 15 minutes then remove the baking beans, brush with egg wash and put back into the oven for a further five minutes. Remove the tart case from the oven, set aside and reduce the oven temperature to 180°C/gas mark 4.

To make the tart

1 Trim the asparagus stalks and discard any tough stems. Cut the asparagus in half on an angle. Blanch in boiling water for one minute then refresh in a bowl of cold water. Drain and pat dry with kitchen roll.

2 Place smoked salmon slices over the bottom of the tart. Scatter over the asparagus and brie. Mix together the eggs, yolks, cream, milk and lemon zest. Season with salt.

3 Pour the egg mixture over the tart until just below the rim. Bake in the oven for 20 minutes until golden. Remove and cool slightly before serving.

Chorizo, wild garlic and Godminster Brie with Cracked Black Pepper croquettes and lemon aioli

Ingredients

750g floury potatoes
100g chorizo
50g wild garlic leaves, washed
1 tbsp butter
50g Godminster Brie with Cracked Black Pepper
1 tsp cayenne pepper
2 eggs, beaten
150g Panko breadcrumbs
Plain flour for dusting
Sunflower oil for frying
Salt and pepper

For the lemon aioli

1 small garlic clove, minced
2 large egg yolks
1 tsp Dijon mustard
100ml extra-virgin olive oil
100ml sunflower oil
Zest of 1 small lemon
Lemon juice to taste
Salt and pepper

To make the lemon aioli

Mix the oils together in a jug. Put the egg yolks, mustard and a squeeze of lemon juice into a bowl and blend using a hand-held blender. Slowly drizzle the oils into the mixture until thick and a pale yellow. Add the garlic, lemon zest and season with salt and pepper. Add a squeeze of lemon juice to thin the mixture down if necessary.

To make the croquettes

1 Peel the potatoes, cut into small chunks and put into a saucepan. Cover with water, add a little salt and bring to the boil. Cook until tender: for about 12 to 15 minutes. Drain in a colander and leave to stand for a few minutes.

2 Chop the chorizo into small dice. Cut the wild garlic leaves in half down the middle, then roughly slice.

3 Once the potatoes are cooked, return them to the pan with the butter, season with salt and pepper and mash until smooth. Stir the chorizo and wild garlic through the mash and chill in the fridge for at least 30 minutes to allow the mixture to firm up.

4 Put the flour and cayenne pepper, along with a pinch of salt, into a bowl. In another bowl add the beaten eggs and in a third bowl add the Panko breadcrumbs.

5 Take a tablespoon of the potato mixture and press a piece of brie into the centre. Roll into a cylinder shape and coat in the flour, shaking off any excess. Then dip into the egg wash, allowing the excess egg to drip back into the bowl before coating the croquette in the Panko breadcrumbs. Repeat with the remaining mixture until you have 12 equal-sized portions.

Continued on page 49...

6 Heat some light oil in a large saucepan. The oil is hot enough when a piece of Panko browns within a minute or so. Once the oil is hot, carefully place the croquettes into the pan and cook until golden brown. Serve immediately with the lemon aioli.

"I like to unwind from work by strolling around my garden with my chickens!"

Richard Hollingbery, Managing Director and founder of Godminster, Bruton

"We are best known for our organic cheese but we also create a range of artisan food inspired by the flavours that can be found at Godminster Farm. When sourcing ingredients, it's important to follow the provenance and go for the best. It's worth paying a little extra for the freshest and highest quality produce.

The best part of my job is seeing people enjoy the cheese as much as they do. The worst part is the paperwork! My proudest moment was definitely when we first turned organic after years of hard work and produced our first cheeses. It's exciting planning for the future and it's great to see plans blossom and come to fruition. The most dangerous farming experience I've had is from a few years back when I accidentally tipped over a trailer of bales on a steep hillside – luckily the tow hitch wasn't capped and the trailer snapped away otherwise it would have pulled the tractor (and me!) along with it.

I like to unwind from work by strolling around my garden with my chickens!"

"When sourcing ingredients, it's important to follow the provenance and go for the best. It's worth paying a little extra for the freshest and highest quality produce."

Dorset

Lemon pots with raspberry sauce and meringue, using Rebecca's Kitchen Lemon Curd

Recipe by David Jones, Chef, Worth Matravers Tea & Supper Room, Worth Matravers

Prepare the meringues in advance

For the meringues
2 large egg whites
70g unrefined caster sugar

For the lemon pots
200ml Rebecca's Kitchen Lemon Curd
100ml greek-style yoghurt
100ml crème fraîche
Zest of 1 small lemon
3g sheet of gelatin

For the raspberry sauce
250g fresh raspberries
Juice of half a small lemon
2 heaped tbsp icing sugar

Top Tip: Replace the raspberries with any other soft fruit you fancy for a variation on this simple recipe.

To make the meringues
1 Pre-heat the oven to 200°C/gas mark 6. Whisk the egg whites with an electric whisk at full speed until they resemble soft peaks. Turn the whisk down to the slowest setting and slowly add the caster sugar.
2 When fully combined, divide the mixture into four on a baking sheet and place in the oven. Immediately turn the temperature down to 140°C/gas mark 1.
3 After 40 minutes, turn the oven off and open the door, leaving it ajar for about an hour before removing the lightly coloured meringues.

To make the lemon pots
1 Cover the gelatin in cold water and soak for five minutes.
2 Meanwhile whisk together the remaining ingredients.
3 With your hands, gently squeeze the gelatin to extract any excess liquid then put it into another bowl with a few drops of boiling water. Stir to completely dissolve the gelatin, adding more drops of boiling water if necessary.
4 Add this to the lemon curd mix and stir continuously with the whisk until the ingredients are combined.
5 Divide into four glasses and set in the fridge for an hour.

To serve
1 Blitz the raspberries, lemon juice and icing sugar in a blender, then press through a fine sieve.
2 Dress the lemon pots with raspberry sauce and top with the meringues. There should be plenty of raspberry sauce left to use another day!

David Jones, Chef, Worth Matravers Tea & Supper Room, Worth Matravers

"Along with my wife, Diana, I own the vintage Worth Matravers Tea & Supper Room in Dorset. I don't like sickly sweet desserts – personally I like them rich and tart – so when I was presented with the delightful Rebecca's Kitchen Lemon Curd I was totally inspired to make the lemon pots with raspberry sauce and meringue.

Diana stocks many of Rebecca's other jams and chutneys in her deli in Swanage and they are the perfect accompaniment to the organic scones we serve at the Tea Room. We are so lucky to live in an area where beautiful ingredients are to be found almost upon our doorstep. We use local Cedar Organic Eggs in our recipes and even flour milled in Dorset!

Living in the beautiful coastal village of Worth Matravers, I love nothing more than a stroll up the road for a pint of real ale at my local pub, The Square & Compass, where I can chat with the locals and unwind from the hectic hubbub of the busy kitchen at the Tea Room."

Dorset Lobster mac and cheese with Palmers Best Bitter sauce

Recipe by Jean-Paul De Ronne, Head Chef, Anchor Inn, Seatown

Ingredients

Meat from 2 cooked lobsters
(available from most fishmongers)
150g macaroni, cooked
30g hazelnuts, crushed and toasted
25g breadcrumbs
25g cheddar cheese, grated

For the sauce

100g cheddar cheese, grated
100g Dorset Blue Vinny
125ml Palmers Best Bitter,
Traditional IPA
1 tsp English mustard
75g breadcrumbs
50g plain flour
25ml Dorsetshire Sauce (or
Worcestershire sauce)
2 tsp Thai fish sauce
2 eggs, plus 2 egg yolks
250ml double cream
Salt to taste

To make the sauce

1 Place the cheddar, bitter and mustard into a cold pan over a low heat. The cheese should melt but if it gets too hot it will split and separate the fat, so keep a close eye!

2 As soon as the cheese has softened to a silken puddle, add the breadcrumbs and flour and stir in with a wooden or rubber spatula until all the ingredients have bound together. Continue to cook out on a low heat until the mix forms a ball.

3 Remove from heat and place into a cold bowl or plate to cool for five minutes.

4 Place the cheese mixture into a food processor, add the Dorsetshire Sauce, fish sauce, eggs and additional yolks and blend on high speed until smooth and spreadable.

5 With the blender on a low speed, add the cream, mixing it evenly into the cheese base.

To serve

1 In a clean bowl, place the cooked lobster (chopped into chunky pieces) and 15g of the hazelnuts, a pinch of salt and the macaroni. Add the cheese sauce and combine the ingredients evenly.

2 Divvy up the mix between four ovenproof dishes. Top with the remaining hazelnuts, breadcrumbs and cheddar. Place in a pre-heated oven (180°C/gas mark 4) for 12 to 15 minutes or until golden topped.

3 Serve with a fresh and crisp salad, crusty bread and accompany with a perfectly matched Palmers IPA.

"When creating this dish, be bold and try different ideas."

Jean-Paul De Ronne

Jean-Paul De Ronne, Head Chef, Anchor Inn, Seatown

"I drew inspiration for this dish from many things about this county but, in particular, this pub that attracted me to work here in the initial instance. The ingredients and produce available around here are great. Dorset really has the cream of the crop, and that is what I need for the food I like to create – the best and freshest available.

Having previously matched Palmers' ales with food for a 'Meet the Maker' evening at the Anchor Inn, I expanded my take on a laden Dorset rarebit to create this lobster mac and cheese using Palmers Best IPA. The notes of the ale really help lift the finished dish, blending with all the other layers of flavours and making it a perfect meal for a summer's day.

When creating this dish, be bold and try different ideas. In the spring I like to add wild garlic to the sauce, sometimes I will use the lobster and sauce for a tagliatelle or linguine. Even a hit of truffle at the end gives this dish extra oomph."

Darren Batten, Head Brewer & Director, Palmers Brewery, Bridport

"We brew a range of cask ales and bottled ales to supply our own estate of tenanted pubs throughout Dorset, Somerset and Devon. We also sell to pubs, bars, shops and restaurants around England.

JP at The Anchor is Head Chef at one of our flagship tenanted pubs. We have worked together previously.

We source the best ingredients for our ales (Maris Otter barley and East Kent Golding hops). We will always buy on quality rather than price as the best raw materials make the best real ales.

The best part of my job is designing new seasonal ales from an idea all the way to drinking the final product. I don't really have a worst part, but it can be very demanding ensuring we don't run out of stock in busy trading periods. I do a lot of buying for the brewery and have to predict what we are going to sell a couple of weeks in advance!"

Chesil Smokery Smoked Duck Salad with blackberry ketchup

Recipe by Gordon 'Gordie' Sutherland, Chef Proprietor, Moreton Tearooms, Moreton, Dorchester

Ingredients

2 Chesil Smokery Smoked Duck breasts (you may have a bit left over to use as chef's tasties!)
2 salsify
½ a lemon
Rapeseed or vegetable oil for deep frying
1 courgette
200g mixed leaves (preferably rocket or watercress)
A few sprigs of dill
2 tbsp smoked rapeseed oil
2 tbsp pomegranate molasses
Edible flowers to decorate (optional)

For the blackberry ketchup

500g blackberries
50g caster sugar
15g salt
60ml cider vinegar
4 juniper berries
1 shallot, roughly chopped
1 bay leaf
2g agar agar (optional)

This will make more than you need but will keep in a bottle in the fridge for a couple of weeks.

To make the ketchup (this can be done days in advance)

1 Put the blackberries, sugar, salt, vinegar, juniper berries, shallot and bay leaf in a medium-sized pan, and bring to the boil.
2 Reduce the heat and simmer for 10 to 15 minutes until the liquid has reduced by half.
3 Remove from the heat and pass through a fine sieve, pushing through as much of the berry pulp as you can.
4 Return the mixture to the heat, bring to the boil then sprinkle with the agar agar.
5 Simmer for one to two minutes until the agar agar is absorbed (if you reduce it down too far, add a dash of water).
6 Remove from the heat and pass through the sieve again to remove any undissolved lumps of agar agar. Allow to set in a cool place for around 30 minutes then blitz in a food processor until smooth. Spoon into a squeezy bottle for perfect presentation.

For the salsify crisps

1 Peel the salsify and immediately ribbon with a peeler into water and lemon juice to prevent discoloration.
2 Remove from the water and pat dry with kitchen paper.
3 Deep-fry at 180°C for one minute until lightly brown. Drain on kitchen paper.

For the salad

1 Ribbon the courgette with a peeler. Blanch for 30 seconds in boiling water, then refresh in ice-cold water. Remove from the water, pat dry with kitchen paper and roll into cylinders.

Continued on page 65 ...

2 Slice the duck breast thinly – be careful not to go too thin as it will fall apart. Roll the slices into cylinders.

3 Shake the smoked rapeseed oil and pomegranate molasses together in a jar.

4 Arrange the duck breast, courgette, salsify crisps and blackberry ketchup on four plates, finishing with a drizzle of the molasses mix, the dill and some edible flowers.

Top Tip: Wear gloves when peeling the salsify.

Gordon 'Gordie' Sutherland, Chef Proprietor, Moreton Tearooms, Moreton, Dorchester

"This duck recipe has been re-created at the Tearooms, as well as at weddings on a multiple scale, in various guises, since the autumn when we had a glut of blackberries. The subtle smoking of the duck and the sharpness of the blackberries seem to complement each well. Apart from the duck, I love the sweet earthiness of the salsify.

We have used Chesil Smokery products for a number of years now. We are like-minded in our thinking, using the best products available, local wherever possible, to produce the best, fairly priced food.

Having such a plethora of fantastic producers and ingredients right here in the West Country is the best thing about my job, as is being my own boss. Which is also the worst thing about my job!

I like to unwind by shooting duck and picking blackberries! The latter with my children who eat more than they carry. Lately my midlife crisis has involved taking up trail running and I recently came last in my first half marathon!"

Sea bass with sizzled ginger, chilli and spring onions, served with Watercress Company Baby Leaf Salad

Recipe by Jackie Spendlow, Sladers Yard Licensed Café, West Bay, Bridport

Ingredients

8 sea bass fillets, skin on and scaled
4 tbsp sunflower oil
Large knob of ginger, peeled and
    shredded into matchsticks
4 garlic cloves, thinly sliced
4 fat, fresh red chillis, deseeded and
    thinly shredded
12 to 16 spring onions, shredded
    lengthways
4 tsp soy sauce
Baby leaf salad
Lime to serve

Method

1   Heat three tablespoons of oil and gently fry the ginger, garlic and chilli until golden. Remove from the pan, toss in the spring onions and set aside.

2   Season the sea bass fillets with salt and pepper and slash the skin three times. Add one tablespoon of oil to the frying pan and once hot, fry the fish skin side down for five minutes, or until the skin is crisp. Turn and cook for another 30 seconds to a minute.

3   Splash the fish with a little soy sauce and spoon over the ginger, chilli and spring onion mixture. Serve on a bed of baby leaves with slices of lime.

"We like to give our customers a genuine coastal treat"

Jackie Spendlow, Sladers Yard Licensed Café, West Bay, Bridport

"Fish is my favourite ingredient. Sustainable of course. Using fresh, local and healthy ingredients is really important to us. We like to give our customers a genuine coastal treat. The sea bass used in this recipe is caught near to us, just off Chesil Beach, so it's great to use. The sizzled ginger, spring onion and soy sauce make it just that extra bit special. You can't go wrong if you only use very fresh, high-quality ingredients.

I love the interaction with the customers who come specifically for the whole experience – to see the art in our gallery and enjoy the food – so it's always interesting. We're learning all the time and that's brilliant. It's always a satisfying and proud moment seeing someone celebrating a special occasion with one of our individually designed menus – a really happy bride is wonderful!

Working at Sladers Yard, I don't ever get wound up! It's such a pleasure working here. I mean it!"

Devon

Mediterranean Sharpham Ticklemore Goat cheese slice

Recipe by Sue Hudson, partner Ashburton Delicatessen

Ingredients

325g all-butter puff pastry, ready rolled
20g semi-dried sun blush tomatoes
6 pitted green olives, halved
30g grilled sliced aubergines or courgettes, drained and cut into strips
80g roasted red peppers, drained and cut into strips
Half a grilled artichoke heart, cut into strips
A twist of black pepper
100g Sharpham Ticklemore Goat cheese
1 egg, lightly beaten
Parsley, chopped

Method

1 Preheat the oven to 180°C/gas mark 4. Divide the rolled pastry into four rectangles. Egg-wash a border of about 1cm around the edges of each rectangle – not in the middle.
2 Arrange the chopped vegetables in the centre of each portion of pastry, avoiding the egg-washed area.
3 Crumble the cheese over the top of the vegetables and season with pepper.
4 Bake in the preheated oven for eight to ten minutes or until puffed up around the edges and golden brown. Garnish with chopped parsley.

Sue Hudson, partner with son Robin Hudson, Ashburton Delicatessen, Ashburton

"Our dish of Mediterranean slice is based on Spanish Coca and has Sharpham Ticklemore Goat cheese on top. We bake these fresh in the shop every day and they are very popular.

We stock between 50 and 60 different cheeses (including seven made by Sharpham Estates), as well as regional charcuterie, preserves, biscuits, cakes, ice cream and even award-winning falafel from Bristol!

When sourcing ingredients I look for three things: taste (all-important, obviously), provenance and packaging – the best product can fail due to poor packaging.

To unwind, I love to walk my dogs on beautiful Dartmoor."

Mark Sharman, Managing Director, cheesemaker and winemaker, Sharpham Wine and Cheese, Ashprington, Totnes

"We've been supplying the national independent trade and specialist food service with wine and cheese since 1981, a very fast 35 years! We use milk from our own Jersey herd, established in 1952, to make a range of luxury soft cheeses and grow grapes on the farm to produce excellent examples of English wine.

When sourcing ingredients buy them from people you know well and who know what they are doing. For example, we buy goats' milk that has been produced on the same farm for 29 years – they are dedicated to producing the best quality milk. This sort of ingredient makes cheesemaking a joy!

One of the best parts of my job is arriving at 5:30 on a May morning when the sun is shining and the birds are singing. One of the worst is arriving at 5:30 on a January morning when it is freezing cold and lashing with rain!"

Gazpacho soup with Favis of Salcombe crab

Recipe by Franck Favereaux, Head Chef, Otterton Mill, Otterton

For the gazpacho

600g ripe cherry tomatoes
250g cucumber, peeled, deseeded and diced
250g green pepper, deseeded and diced
1 large onion
2 garlic bulbs
2 tbsp balsamic vinegar
2 tsp demerara sugar
100ml olive oil
Ground salt and pepper

For the crab

2 egg yolks
1 tbsp white-wine vinegar
1 tsp wholegrain mustard
200ml olive oil
200g white crab meat
4 large ripe tomatoes
40g cucumber, diced
20g chives, chopped
20g coriander, chopped
Juice of 1 lime
Ground salt and pepper

For the garnish

Micro herbs
Olive oil

Method

1 Blitz all the gazpacho ingredients in a blender, adding water if it's too thick. Season to taste, then strain through a fine sieve and chill for a couple of hours.

2 Make the mayonnaise for the crab by beating together the egg yolks, wholegrain mustard and vinegar with an electric mixer. With the mixer on slow, gradually add the olive oil until the mixture thickens. Season to taste.

3 Put the tomatoes in boiling water for one minute. Remove and transfer briefly to a bowl of iced water. Drain, then remove the skin. Cut the tomatoes in half from top to bottom, remove the seeds then use a cutter to cut a circle from each half. Dice the remaining tomato.

4 Mix the crab with the diced tomatoes, diced cucumber, chives, coriander and lime juice. Add the wholegrain mustard mayonnaise and season.

5 To dress, place a round cutter in the centre of a soup bowl. Place one of the tomato circles inside, place a good layer of crab on top pressing down then add another tomato circle and build to the top of the cutter. Remove the cutter carefully.

6 Pour the chilled gazpacho around the tower, top the crab with micro herbs and drizzle with a little olive oil.

Franck Favereaux, Head Chef, Otterton Mill, Otterton

"With a deep knowledge of ingredients, I love perfection and simplicity. This dish is inspired by the light, cool summer flavours of the gazpacho and the delicate flavour of the crab, all too often lost in other dishes.

We use a lot of crab in the spring and summer months and the quality of Favis' is one we highly recommend. Seasoning is crucial with this dish and ensures the delicate flavours are not lost. Crab is such a fabulous ingredient. As a chef who has worked with seafood the whole of my career I appreciate its versatile qualities: use it in a crab bisque or a simple sandwich! My top cooking tip is to season your food and taste, the dish should leave the kitchen as a finished plate.

Working at Otterton Mill is special. We are a small team operating in the beautiful natural environment of the River Otter that flows alongside the kitchen. That beats the hustle and bustle of a city kitchen, any day.

I unwind from work spending time with my wife Sarah and our two children William and Lottie. I am also a coach of a local youth football team: the Arsene Wenger of The Lympstone Lions!"

Kevin Favis, Director, Favis of Salcombe

"We had never worked with Franck Favereaux before, but we are very excited by the dish he created with our product – it looked amazing!

We fish for sustainable crab and lobster off the Devon coast and supply to local businesses in Devon, as well as to restaurants in London, Manchester and Birmingham. You should always go for the freshest product with a known provenance – we pride ourselves on delivering handpicked crab, where the only tools used to extract the meat are a teaspoon and a mallet.

Highlights of my job include people telling me how ours is the best crab they've ever tasted and how there's never any shell in it. Also the fact that almost my entire family is involved in the business is pretty great. We take great pride in our beautiful boat, the *Emma Jane SE101*.

I'm happiest when pedalling around the South Hams' lanes, training to compete in road races. I also enjoy riding my big Irish Draft Cross Thoroughbred mare, Holly or Big H, as she's known. My horsey friends call me Crabman. Actually, quite a few people call me Crabman... but then I guess I am!"

Favis of Salcombe crab benedict with blanched asparagus

Recipe by Rudi Bell, Sous Chef, Dukes, Sidmouth

Ingredients
4 free-range eggs
A dash of white wine vinegar
4 English muffins
8 asparagus spears

For the crab
500g brown crab meat
200g white crab meat
2 tbsp mayonnaise
2 tsp lemon juice
Salt and pepper

For the hollandaise sauce
6 free-range egg yolks
2 small shallots peeled and sliced
2 bay leaves
4 white peppercorns
2 sprigs of tarragon
200ml white-wine vinegar
250g unsalted butter, melted

To make the hollandaise sauce
1. Reduce the white-wine vinegar in a pan with the shallots, tarragon, bay leaves and white peppercorns. Once reduced, strain through a fine sieve, set aside the liquid and discard the other ingredients.
2. Place the egg yolks in a heat-proof bowl set over a pan of simmering water, whisking until soft and fluffy.
3. Continue whisking and slowly pour the melted butter into the yolks. When the mix has thickened add the reduced vinegar to taste and check the seasoning. Remove the bowl from the pan of water, cover with cling film and set aside in a warm place.

Method
1. Mix the brown crab meat into the mayonnaise until smooth, then add the white crab meat, lemon juice and season to taste.
2. Boil a pan of water, add a pinch of salt and blanch the asparagus spears for four minutes.
3. At the same time, poach the eggs. Bring a saucepan of water to the boil with a dash of white-wine vinegar. Swirl the water around using a whisk then add the eggs and poach for around four minutes.
4. While the eggs are poaching, toast the English muffins until golden.
5. When the eggs are done, take out and drain on kitchen paper. Drain the asparagus.
6. Place the muffins onto plates, divide the crab mix between them, top with poached eggs, spoon the hollandaise over the eggs and serve the asparagus on the side.

"Seasoning can make or break a dish, so always taste what you are making so you can get it just right."

Rudi Bell, Sous Chef, Dukes, Sidmouth

"The inspiration for this dish was actually my kids who wanted to make something special for their mum on Mother's Day. After much discussion we agreed there's nothing mum loves more than crab and poached eggs. The most important thing to consider when making a good crab benedict is the quality of the ingredients. Luckily living by the seaside and with many good local suppliers, I was laughing.

Seasoning can make or break a dish, so always taste what you are making so you can get it just right.

Getting to try new things is the best part of my job. The worst part would be the late hours, but having a great local cider with the team after work helps us unwind.

I must say winning gold in the Taste of the West Awards and bronze in the Devon Tourism Awards last year for Pub of the Year are two of my prouder moments."

"The inspiration for this dish was actually my kids who wanted to make something special for their mum on Mother's Day. After much discussion we agreed there's nothing mum loves more than crab and poached eggs."

South Devon Chilli Farm chocolate fondant

Recipe by David Jenkins, Chef and Owner,
Rock Salt Café and Brasserie, Plymouth

Ingredients

64g caster sugar

2 large eggs

70g egg yolk

125g unsalted butter, plus a little extra for greasing

125g South Devon Chilli Farm Madagascar 70% Dark Chilli Chocolate

36g plain flour

2 tsp cocoa powder

Method

1 Preheat the oven to 200°C/gas mark 6. Brush four individual pudding moulds with melted butter, refrigerate until set, then brush again with melted butter. Add a half a teaspoon of cocoa powder to each mould, swirling it around so the powder completely coats all sides of the mould. Tip out any excess.

2 Melt the chocolate and butter together in a microwave, or over a bain marie. Once melted, leave to cool for 10 minutes.

3 In a separate bowl, whisk the eggs, yolks and sugar together until thick, pale and doubled in size. Fold in the sifted flour, then the cooled, melted butter and chocolate. Make sure the mixture is thoroughly combined to a loose batter.

4 Divide the mixture between the pudding moulds and chill for at least 20 minutes.

5 Cook in the preheated oven for 10 to 12 minutes, or until the tops have formed a crust and the fondant is starting to come away from the sides of the mould. Leave to rest for at least two minutes before turning out.

6 Delicious served with passion fruit syrup, sorbet, crème fraîche sorbet or Thai basil and toasted coconut.

Top Tip: I recommend scaling this recipe up to allow for any puddings that collapse. If you have any leftover, the mixture freezes perfectly for next time.

> "A fun part of our job is watching people playing Russian Roulette with our Pimiento de Padron chillies (one in every six is hot!)"
>
> Kaz Lobendhan

David Jenkins, Chef and Owner, Rock Salt Café and Brasserie, Plymouth

"Chocolate fondants have always been a show-stopper for dinner parties, and using chilli chocolate gave me a chance to combine my passion for Asian food with this classic dessert. Surprisingly we hadn't worked with South Devon Chilli Farm before but chilli is such a strong part of this recipe we were excited at the chance to create something new! We will definitely be working together in the future.

Resting the fondant is very important as it helps to form the outer shell that holds the liquid centre.

Being a chef means long and unsociable hours but the buzz of working with great local ingredients to create the perfect dish that people appreciate, there's nothing better! My most exciting moment has to be the first day I opened Rock Salt, and to do it with my family, that would definitely have to be my proudest moment. The staff has grown with me in the business and is now a big part of helping me run two family restaurants."

Kaz Lobendhan, Owner and Director, South Devon Chilli Farm, Loddiswell

"I am one of four owners/directors – Steve, Heather and Martin are my fellow chilli heads. We grow tonnes of chillies each year here on the farm – lots of different varieties in a range of heats. We have a display tunnel with around 200 different varieties that is open to the public from June to December. Most of our crop is processed on-site in our commercial kitchen to produce chilli preserves, chilli sauces and chilli chocolates. We sell all of our products in our farm shop and nationwide via our online shop. We supply wholesale to farm shops and delis throughout Europe.

The best parts of our job are sharing our passion for chillies with customers and introducing them to new flavours and chillies they have never heard of. We love getting people hooked on the endorphin rush you get with chilli heat in the delicious flavours of our chilli jam and chilli chocolates. Plus, watching brave people push themselves to try our hottest sauces, with mouth-tingling consequences – we stand by with a glass of milk to cool the fire!"

Sharpham Cremet and Jerusalem artichoke risotto

Recipe by David Jenkins, Chef and Owner,
Rock Salt Café and Brasserie, Plymouth

Ingredients

200g Sharpham Cremet (an artisan goats' cheese enriched with cream)
60g yellow chanterelle mushrooms
150g Jerusalem artichokes, peeled and diced
700ml vegetable stock
50g butter
150g arborio risotto rice
2 shallots, finely diced
50g Parmesan cheese, finely grated
30g candied walnuts, chopped
15g fresh black truffle

Top Tip: It's important to keep the risotto moving while cooking – this ensures the grains of rice cook evenly and stops it from getting stodgy. This dish works all year round, try replacing the artichokes with asparagus or celery and grapes.

Method

1 Start by part-cooking the risotto. Warm 350ml of vegetable stock in a pan. In a separate heavy-based pan warm 25g of butter until melted, add the shallots and allow them to sweat for two to three minutes until soft.
2 Add the arborio rice to the shallots and cook for a minute, stirring. Add a ladle of stock and reduce the heat to a bare simmer, stirring continuously until the stock has been absorbed. Continue adding stock until it has all been incorporated. The rice should still be al dente.
3 Tip the rice onto a tray, cover and leave to cool.

To serve

1 Warm the remaining 350ml of stock. Cut the Cremet into eight thin slices and set aside.
2 In a large, heavy-based saucepan, melt the remaining 25g butter and sauté the artichokes for three minutes. Add the chanterelles and a pinch of salt and cook until softened.
3 Add the precooked rice to the pan with the vegetables, stirring in a ladle of hot stock. Cook, stirring until the stock has been absorbed by the rice. Continue the process until nearly all the stock has been added or the rice is very nearly cooked, it should be just a little al dente.
4 Add the grated Parmesan, taste the risotto and season if required. Add a little stock or butter if it seems dry or lacking in richness.
5 Divide the risotto into four shallow bowls. Place two slices of Cremet on each bowl.
6 Warm briefly under a pre-heated grill and garnish with candied walnuts and grated black truffle.

Coronation brown shrimp with spiced pineapple chutney, using Otter Vale Coronation Sauce

Recipe by Chris Dayer, Head Chef, River Exe Cafe, Exmouth

For the shrimp
2 tbsp Otter Vale Coronation Sauce
200g brown shrimp
2 tbsp seasoned flour
1 egg, beaten
150g breadcrumbs
Vegetable oil, for frying

For the pineapple chutney
½ tsp fresh ginger
1 small white onion
1 red chilli
½ a fresh pineapple
100g granulated sugar
100g white-wine vinegar

To make the shrimp
1 Mix the Coronation Sauce with the shrimp to bind.
2 Place a sheet of cling film onto a work surface and spoon the shrimp onto it. Roll into a tight cylinder, secure at each end and freeze for two hours.
3 After two hours, remove the roll from the freezer and cut into four equal portions, removing the cling film. Roll each portion in the flour, dust off and dip into the beaten eggs, then coat in the breadcrumbs. For a deeper crust, re-dip the rolled shrimp into the beaten eggs and breadcrumbs, missing out the flour. Chill in the fridge until you are almost ready to serve.

To make the pineapple chutney
1 Chop the ginger, onion and chilli. In a saucepan add a splash of olive oil and place over a medium heat. Add the chopped ingredients and sweat until soft but not golden. Finely dice the pineapple, season and add to the pan and cook down for three to four minutes.
2 Add the sugar and simmer until it's dissolved. Add the white-wine vinegar and simmer until the liquid is reduced to a syrup.

To serve
Deep fry the breaded shrimp until a light golden brown, plate and serve with the spiced chutney.

Roasted breast of duck, charred chicory with fig and date jus, using Otter Vale jelly and relish

Recipe by Chris Dayer, Head Chef, River Exe Cafe, Exmouth

Ingredients
2 duck breasts
4 tsp Otter Vale Redcurrant, Mint and
  Orange Jelly

For the fig and date jus
2 shallots
1 carrot
1 leek
2 cloves of garlic
1 stick of celery
1 sprig of thyme
1 bay leaf
20ml red wine
100ml Port
50ml red-wine vinegar
500ml chicken stock
2 tsp Otter Vale Date and Fig Relish
Vegetable oil

For the Chicory
1 head of chicory
100ml soy sauce
400ml orange juice
50g butter
4 fresh figs

To make the fig and date jus
1 Roughly chop the shallots, carrots, celery, leek and garlic. Add enough vegetable oil to cover the bottom of a medium-sized pan and place over a medium heat until it starts to smoke. Add the chopped vegetables and, keeping them moving, cook until they reach a dark brown colour. Add the thyme, the bay leaf, then the red wine, port and vinegar. Turn down to a low heat and reduce the mixture until very little liquid is remaining. Add in the chicken stock and reduce again by half.
2 Strain through a fine sieve into another pan. Return to the heat and reduce again until syrupy, then add the date and fig relish. If the sauce is too thick, add a splash of water.

For the duck
Season the duck breasts with salt and pepper and place them in a cold frying pan. Bring the pan up to a high heat and cook the duck evenly until both sides are golden brown. Remove the pan from the heat and rest the duck.

For the chicory
Remove any damaged outer leaves then cut the chicory in half, length ways. Sprinkle the chicory with a little caster sugar and caramelise in a hot pan. Add the soy sauce, orange juice and butter, cover with a lid and reduce the heat. Cook for five to six minutes, basting regularly.

Continued on page 99...

To serve

1 Cut the figs in half and place a teaspoon of Otter Vale Redcurrant, Mint and Orange Jelly on each fleshy fruit half. Place under a hot grill to glaze.
2 Slice the duck breasts and plate with the chicory and figs. Pour over the jus.

Chris Dayer, Head Chef, River Exe Cafe, Exmouth

"I love working with local produce and when we were paired with Otter Vale it was a challenge for me to come up with recipes that could combine their produce with my style of cooking. I love a challenge! I wanted to produce a recipe to showcase what we are about at the River Exe Cafe and to bring out the best flavours from Otter Vale. I also wanted to prove that you can produce restaurant-standard food in your own kitchen. I really enjoyed cooking it, and I want the readers to enjoy the experience of cooking too: never rush a recipe.

You should use your senses when cooking – the aroma, how you create the dish and obviously the taste.

I never get tired of someone experiencing the taste of a dish for the first time and being surprised at how much they enjoyed it. That gives me great pleasure.

When I'm not reading through recipe books, which I really enjoy doing, I'm out on the river enjoying life!"

Ben Laxon, Director, Otter Vale Products, Budleigh Salterton

"Our business has been in existence since the late 1970s and run by the family for the past 21 years, during which time we have expanded our range and now supply many of the South West's wonderful farm shops, delis, restaurants, pubs and butchers.

My mum has always been an excellent cook and my earliest memories are of times in the kitchen cooking with her. I never thought I'd grow up making food for a living, but I have discovered a passion for it and it's a joy to produce delicious things for people to eat. Inventing new recipes, at home or work, is an absolute pleasure.

It's sometimes a challenge to keep up with demand, but that means we are doing something right. The West Country is full of wonderful producers and ingredients, and if you can't find what you are looking for locally, then there are a raft of knowledgeable, friendly people who will help you source it.

When I'm not rushing about on behalf of the business, I can be found rushing about a hockey pitch. I have had the honour of representing England at the Masters World Cup in Australia."

Dressed native blue lobster cocktail using Bell & Loxton Rapeseed Oil for the mayonnaise, with fennel, apple & chilli

Recipe by Martin Benjamin, Chef/Proprietor, The Samphire Bush, Plymouth

For the mayonnaise
2 egg yolks
75ml Bell & Loxton Rapeseed Oil
75ml sunflower oil
1 tsp Dijon mustard
Juice of half a lemon
1 tsp white-wine vinegar
1 tbsp cold water
Salt and pepper to taste

For the dressed lobster cocktail
300g native blue lobster meat,
    cooked and diced
1 spring onion, finely sliced
1 tsp parsley, chopped
1 tsp coriander, chopped
Zest and juice of half a lemon
Salt and pepper to taste
Half a fennel bulb, thinly sliced
1 small red apple, thinly sliced
1 small chilli, deseeded and sliced
A few sprigs of coriander cress

Top Tip: Squeeze some lemon juice onto the sliced fennel to stop it going brown.

To make the mayonnaise
1 Combine the egg yolks, lemon juice, Dijon mustard and white-wine vinegar in a bowl and, using an electric mixer, whisk to make a paste.
2 Slowly add half of the rapeseed and sunflower oils. Add a tablespoon of cold water and continue to whisk. Continue adding the remaining oils until the mayonnaise has thickened. Season to taste with salt and pepper.

To make the lobster
Place the cooked lobster meat, chopped parsley, chopped coriander, spring onion, lemon zest and juice into a bowl and mix thoroughly. Add enough of the rapeseed mayonnaise to loosely bind all the ingredients. The seasoning may have been diluted by the lobster meat, so taste and season again if necessary.

To serve
1 Place a medium-sized pastry cutter onto a plate and spoon a portion of the lobster cocktail into it, pressing gently to form a patty shape. Repeat for the remaining three portions.
2 Place a few slices of apple on top of each portion of lobster, then top with the fennel and chilli. Put some of the remaining mayonnaise into a squeezy bottle and squeeze equally-spaced dots of mayonnaise around the dish. Dress with a sprig of cress on each mayonnaise dot.

Martin Benjamin, Chef/Proprietor, The Samphire Bush, Plymouth

"Having been a chef for just shy of 20 years I have to say that fresh British produce is something to shout about year after year. As the seasons change, what we create using local produce changes, too. Although we all melt back into some of our favourite methods of using them – for example, one year we might be inspired to make elderflower panna cotta then the following year we might be inspired to make elderflower jelly – who knows where our ideas and inspirations will lead to next? But if we stay in the game then we'll find out and be able to educate and share our passion with others. I haven't worked with Bell & Loxton before but after using their product in this recipe, they might have just earned themselves a new customer!

The best part of my job is that I can cook whatever I want. The worst part is slogging it out in a hot kitchen in the summer – gets a bit toasty sometimes! Though I'm always proud to create a dish that our customers enjoy. It's what makes life worthwhile in a hot kitchen."

Jonathan Bell, Bell & Loxton, Kingsbridge

"Since 2010 we've been producing award-winning, cold-pressed rapeseed oil with rape grown, pressed and bottled on the family farm in the heart of South Devon. The oil is stocked throughout Devon in many farm shops and delicatessens, as well as in regional Waitrose stores in Devon, Cornwall, Dorset and Somerset.

Our original rapeseed oil was awarded 3 stars by the Great Taste Awards in 2013 and named in the Top 50 products nationwide, the only rapeseed oil to have achieved this. We launched our flavoured oils in 2015 which have also proved very popular.

I love meeting customers at food fairs to talk about how the oil is made and discuss all its benefits! Working long hours means that I have very little 'free time' but when I do I enjoy watching rugby and spending time cycling with the family."

Smoked ham hock & Quicke's Mature Cheddar terrine with Jail Ale pickled onion, cheese toasty and cheese beignet

Recipe by Mike Palmer, Executive Chef, Two Bridges Hotel, Dartmoor and The Bedford Hotel, Tavistock

For the terrine
2 ham hocks
1 tsp coarse-grain mustard
60g shiitake mushrooms, sliced
10 spring onions or baby leeks
1 gelatin leaf
250ml pork stock (made by cooking the meat with leek, celery, garlic, onion, thyme and peppercorns)
250g Quicke's Mature Cheddar
Wild garlic to wrap (if unavailable, use leeks or spring cabbage)

For the toasty
Butter
2 slices white bread
1 tsp olive oil
A good handful of Quicke's Mature Cheddar

For the pickled onions
50ml pickling vinegar
50g sugar
50ml Dartmoor Brewery Jail Ale
6 pickling onions

For the beignet
50g butter
75ml water
40g flour
50g Quicke's Mature Cheddar
1 free-range egg
Sosa Airbag Farina (pork scratching granules) or breadcrumbs, to coat

To make the pickled onions
1 Peel and clean the pickling onions and put them into a jar.
2 Bring all the wet ingredients to the boil in a saucepan, then pour while hot over the onions and seal the jar.

Note: This will make a whole jar of pickles. These will keep and I suggest preparing them as far in advance as possible.

To make the terrine
3 Soak the ham hocks overnight in cold water to extract some of the salt. Discard the salty water and add the hocks to a fresh pan of cold water with diced leek, celery, garlic, onion, thyme and peppercorns. Braise in the oven at 150°c/gas mark 2 (or in a slow cooker) for a minimum of four hours, until the meat is falling off the bone.

Continued on page 108...

4 Allow the meat to cool, then drain, reserving the cooking liquor. Depending on the taste, you may need to reduce it by half, or until full flavour is reached. Be careful, as if over-reduced the stock may become salty.

5 Soak one gelatin leaf in cold water, then add to 250ml of the hot stock. Mix with the meat and mustard – this mixture should feel damp to touch.

6 Cook the spring onions in boiling water for around three to four minutes until al denté, then refresh in cold water.

7 Fry the sliced shiitake mushrooms in butter for three to four minutes until evenly coloured and cooked through.

8 Slice the Cheddar into 1cm slices, enough for three layers.

9 Line a terrine or small loaf tin, first with cling film and then with the wild garlic (or leeks or cabbage). Ensure you leave enough cling film and wild garlic to fold over the top of the terrine when the tin is full. Add a layer of the ham mix, then place the cheese slices on top, leaving space around the edges. Add another layer of meat, sealing around the cheese. Follow with a layer of mushrooms and onions.

Continue the sequence until the tin is full. Wrap the wild garlic and cling film over the top, ensuring it's tightly sealed. Weigh the terrine down in the tin and press overnight in the fridge.

To make the toasty
1 Heavily butter both sides of each piece of bread.
2 Grate the cheese and generously layer on top of the bread. Add the second piece of bread and press firmly so the sandwich sticks together. Chill for 10 minutes.
3 Pre-heat the olive oil in a frying pan then fry the sandwich over a medium heat until golden brown on each side. Allow to cool slightly before removing the crusts and slicing into four fingers.

To make the beignet
1 Bring the water and butter to the boil. Stir in the flour, then the egg, then the cheese, mixing thoroughly.
2 Roll into four balls and chill.
3 Coat in Sosa Airbag Farina or breadcrumbs.
4 Deep fry until crispy on the outside.

Mary Quicke, Managing Director, Quicke's, Exeter

"We're a dairy farm producing traditional, clothbound cheddar with milk from our own herd. Cheese is supplied via wholesalers to retailers and restaurants nationally and internationally. Our key ingredient is the milk that we produce: we think about breed of cow, what the cows are eating and stage of lactation. Whatever you're cooking it makes sense to understand what your ingredients are, where they come from and what makes the difference to flavour.

The best part of my job is making world-class cheese, selling it around the world and achieving excellence in farming with our great team. Getting my MBE for services to agriculture and cheese was a very proud moment. The worst part of my job is cleaning up when I make mistakes!

I unwind from work by producing interesting flavoured salads and edible flowers in my garden, and surfing, although I'm a fair-weather surfer now."

"My favourite ingredients to cook with are love and butter."

Mike Palmer

Mike Palmer, Executive Chef, Two Bridges Hotel, Dartmoor and The Bedford Hotel, Tavistock

"The inspiration for this recipe comes from the ham and cheese toasties my mother used to make for me when I was a kid – that with a bag of pickled onion monster munch! All the bits can be done in advance so great for a first course or an afternoon bite.

My favourite ingredients to cook with are love and butter. I always recommend using suppliers who love making their products as much as they love selling it – it really inspires me when you see how passionate they are about what they are doing.

This year has been a rewarding year at the Two Bridges. I have a great team behind me, and working with friends, not just employees, makes it all the more fun and fulfilling. The worst part of my job has to be constantly trying new dessert ideas, ha! Actually, I think the only negative is not getting more time with my Boston Terriers."

Levi Frew, Chef de Partie, Two Bridges Hotel, Dartmoor

"The inspiration behind the Banoffee Baked Alaska was to take a dessert that most people have come across, and add a little twist with the Banoffee Pie ice cream from Orange Elephant. When preparing this dish, it's important to make sure the meringue is nice and thick, almost like marshmallow.

For me, the best thing about being a chef at the Two Bridges Hotel is the opportunity to work as part of a really tight-knit team. Working with best mates makes everything more enjoyable. And it's great to be able unwind from work by exploring Dartmoor – such a magical place."

Orange Elephant Banoffee baked alaska

Recipe by Levi Frew, Chef de Partie, Two Bridges Hotel, Two Bridges, Dartmoor

Ingredients
Orange Elephant Banoffee Pie ice cream
½ banana, sliced
1 tsp caster sugar

For the pistachio sponge
200g unsalted butter
200g caster sugar
2 eggs
225g self-raising flour
70g pistachio purée

For the toffee sauce
50g soft brown sugar
40g unsalted butter
100g double cream

For the Italian meringue
200g egg whites
100g golden caster sugar

To make the pistachio sponge
1 Preheat the oven to 170°C/gas mark 3. Beat the sugar and butter together until light and fluffy. Add the eggs, one at a time, ensuring each is fully incorporated before adding the next. Fold in the flour then mix in the pistachio purée.
2 Bake in a greased and lined eight-inch cake tin for 35 minutes, then leave to cool on a wire rack before turning out.

To make the toffee sauce
Using a heavy-based saucepan, melt the sugar and butter together and bring to the boil. After boiling for a few minutes add the cream and stir until fully combined. Leave to cool.

To make the Italian meringue
1 Put the sugar and two tablespoons of warm water into heavy based pan over a low heat, stirring very occasionally. Once all of the sugar has dissolved start increasing the temperature.
2 Whisk the egg whites until they reach a stiff peak. Using a sugar thermometer heat the sugar syrup to 113°C. Slowly pour the hot syrup onto the egg whites, whisking constantly.
3 Keep whisking until the meringue is thick and completely cold, then spoon into a piping bag.

To serve
1 Sprinkle the sliced banana with caster sugar and caramelise with a blow torch or under the grill until golden brown.

Continued on page 115...

2 Cut out a disk of sponge and place in the centre of each plate. Place a scoop of ice cream on the sponge. Pipe the meringue all over the ice cream in small dots, making sure there are no gaps.

3 Brown the meringue with a blow torch, and garnish the plate with caramelised banana and the toffee sauce.

"I rear the young calves in the autumn, so by the time they are milking they have been with us a while, the satisfaction is enormous."

Helen Taverner, Orange Elephant Ice Cream, Exeter

"I'm in partnership with my husband, so I run Orange Elephant Ice Cream, Rob manages the farm and we meet somewhere in the middle! Our son William is also coming back to the business this year.

The only down side of my job is that it can be long hours, but I love the fact I see the product from calf to cone. I rear the young calves in the autumn, so by the time they are milking they have been with us a while, the satisfaction is enormous, and the pleasure in delivering the product to the customer is immense. Lucky me

to love what I do! Farming can be tough, though. My worst moment was injecting the piglets and being at the wrong end at the wrong time – not a great look!

My top tip for sourcing ingredients is never to compromise at all on quality.

Living on the job is pretty challenging, but to unwind from work I love spending time with friends and our children (when they are home!) as well as walking the dogs, cooking and swimming."

Cornwall

Scallops with Kittows Hogs' Pudding

Recipe by Richard du Pille, Head Chef, Duchy of Cornwall Nursery, Lostwithiel

Ingredients
20 scallops (approximately 225g)
220g Kittows Hogs' Pudding
3 tbsp plain flour
1 egg
3 tbsp fresh breadcrumbs
1 apple
500g mixed pea shoots
1 lemon
Olive oil

For the pickled cucumber
½ pint white-wine vinegar
Juice of 1 lemon
100g granulated sugar
1 tsp salt
4 peppercorns
1 clove of garlic
1 cucumber
Sprig of dill

To make the pickled cucumber (do this at least 24 hours in advance)
1 Pour the vinegar and lemon juice into a pan, add the sugar, salt and peppercorns, dissolve the sugar and bring to the boil for a few minutes. Remove from the heat and cool.
2 Chop the garlic, then peel the cucumber (discarding the skin) into ribbons.
3 Pack the cucumber, garlic and dill into a jam jar, pour over the cooled vinegar and close.

To make the apple crisps
Preheat oven to 120°C/gas mark ¼, slice the apple thinly, place on a lined baking tray and bake for approximately 45 minutes to an hour.

To prepare the pudding and scallops
1 Remove the skin from the Hogs' Pudding, cut into 3mm slices, then in half again to make semi-circles.
2 Season, then dip into the flour, dust off, dip into the egg mix, then into the breadcrumbs. Set to one side.
3 Remove the side muscles from the scallops, the black stomach sack and other bits, rinse and pat dry.
4 Trim any pink roe with scissors and set aside to fry with the scallops.

To cook the dish
1 Fry the breaded hogs' pudding.
2 Transfer to a baking a tray and into a pre-heated oven.
3 Place the seasoned scallops into a hot pan, one at a time.

Contiued on page 121...

The first scallop should sizzle on contact. If it doesn't, wait a few seconds until the pan is hotter. Cook the scallops for about two minutes, then flip and cook for a further two minutes. Both sides should be seared golden brown.

To serve

1 Lightly dress the pea-shoot salad with olive oil and place in the centre of the plate. Arrange the scallops and Hogs' Pudding around the shoots.
2 Finish with the apple crisps, a wedge of lemon and a drizzle of olive oil.

Richard du Pille, Head Chef, Duchy of Cornwall Nursery, Lostwithiel

"The inspiration for this dish comes from the classic combination of scallop and black pudding. We know this flavour combination also works with apple, so I thought about how I could adjust the flavour, textures and cooking methods to put a spin on a classic.

I have worked with James Kittow since the Nursery café opened in June 2011. We have a great working relationship that has only strengthened: he knows the quality of ingredients I look for, plus he's a stone's throw away from me.

My favourite ingredient has to be scallops. I just love the flavour, so much so, that I find it hard not to start eating them before I plate up.

I would advise to always get the best ingredients possible and follow the method closely. There are a few cooking techniques required (frying, bread crumbing, pickling, preparing shellfish) and it can be easy to get into a mess, so the key is in the preparation."

James Kittow, Butcher and Grazier, Kilhallon Farm, Par

"We have our own pedigree herd of Red Ruby and Dexter cattle, plus we work closely with a small number of farmers who produce pork, lamb and beef for us. When sourcing ingredients, I'd always recommend going for quality over price.

With over 130 years of rich heritage, I'm proud to have been born into a long line of master butchers. We're passionate about providing only the finest products to restaurants, retailers and families who value top quality meat. Working with our great team is one of the best parts of my job. One of the worst aspects is the long hours and not spending as much time as I would like with my wife and young family. And farming can be dangerous: a calving heifer once got really nasty and nearly killed Ken and myself!

I am the youngest member in Lostwithiel Rotary Club where we meet once a week and enjoy a beer! To unwind I like to walk the dogs around the farm on an evening, checking our Red Ruby and Dexter cattle, perhaps with a can of beer too!"

Twice-baked Cornish Yarg soufflé

Recipe by Tom Hunter, Executive Chef for Red Hotels,
Scarlet Hotel, Mawgan Porth

Ingredients
25g unsalted butter
25g plain flour
1/2 pint milk
80g Cornish Yarg, grated
4 eggs, separated
5g salt
4 tbsp single cream
1 apple
Handful of walnuts
Salad leaves, lightly dressed

Method
1 Melt the butter in a saucepan without allowing it to get too hot. Stir in the flour and cook for a minute or so.
2 Add the milk a little at a time using a whisk to bring the mixture to a smooth sauce.
3 Melt in the cheese. Let the mixture cool slightly before stirring in the egg yolks and salt.
4 Whisk the egg whites to firm peaks. Still using the whisk, beat a third of the whites into the cheese mixture quite vigorously to loosen, then gently fold in the rest of the whites in two stages.
5 Grease four suitable moulds and place a circle of parchment into the bottom of each. Fill the moulds almost to the top with the cheese mixture.
6 Place the moulds into a deep baking tray and fill with warm water so it comes to just over halfway up the moulds. Bake at 180°C/gas mark 4 for 11 minutes. Allow to cool, then remove from the moulds and refrigerate.

To serve
1 Place the soufflés into individual dishes or bowls, add a splash of cream and a sprinkle of cheese.
2 Bake again at 180°C/gas mark 4 for another eight minutes, and serve straight away with some dressed leaves, apples and walnuts.

Top Tip: Use a bain marie when cooking the soufflés, or they won't turn out as light.

Top Tip: Use the best quality ingredients and the freshest free-range eggs.

"Once when I was working in a kitchen in Cornwall, the power went out in the middle of a dinner service... we carried on cooking for the guests by parking a car outside the kitchen window, and shining the lights in so we could see what we were doing!"

Tom Hunter, Executive Chef for Red Hotels, Scarlet Hotel, Mawgan Porth

"One of my favourite restaurants (Sangsters in Elie, Fife in Scotland) serves a cheese soufflé, made with a Scottish cheese. I eat there every time I'm in Scotland, which is a lot, and I like it so much I've adapted the recipe using Cornish Yarg.

I have always used Yarg in dishes while I've been in Cornwall as it has such a good name.

The best part of my job is the people I get to work with — there are some crazy characters in professional kitchens! The worst part is how demanding the job can be at times.

Once when I was working in a kitchen in Cornwall, the power went out in the middle of a dinner service. The gas stayed on, so we carried on cooking for the guests by parking a car outside the kitchen window, and shining the lights in so we could see what we were doing! Fun, but stressful at the same time..."

Catherine Mead, Owner/ Director, Lynher Dairies, Ponsanooth, near Falmouth

"Our small dairy at Ponsanooth is the sole producer of Cornish Yarg and it's a real joy to see great chefs using it in so many different ways. Its low melting point makes it a versatile ingredient, but above all, it's the taste that counts.

We have a fantastically committed team here at Lynher, with everyone working towards a common goal — to make the best cheeses possible. We also make Wild Garlic Yarg and our new cheese, Cornish Kern. Our pleasing clutch of International and British awards tells us we are getting it right. I am Chair of Fifteen Cornwall, Jamie Oliver's transformative food charity, and a member of both the Specialist Cheesemakers Association Committee and the Guilde Internationale des Fromagers. But I do get some days off. Yoga, walking and cycling are my go-to activities to unwind."

Roast Cornish rabbit with Boddington's Berries Blackberry Conserve and fresh blackberries

Recipe by Lee Groves, Head Chef, The Turks Head, Penzance

Ingredients

2 fresh rabbits, legs, shoulders and loin removed (ask your butcher to do this and keep the bones)
12 blackberries
2 tbsp Boddington's Berries Blackberry Conserve
Olive oil
Red wine
Unsalted butter
Salt and ground white pepper

For the stock and rabbit legs

1 Put the rabbit bones, shoulders and legs in a roasting tray and roast in a hot oven for eight minutes.
2 Once roasted, season with salt and pepper and add enough water to the roasting tray to cover the rabbit. Place a sheet of tin foil over the tray, ensuring the edges are tightly sealed. Cook in the oven at 150°C/gas mark 2 for an hour and a half.
3 Remove from the oven, take the legs out of the tray and cover to keep warm. Strain the stock liquid, discarding the bones but keeping the shoulders – they can be frozen for future use in a pie or casserole.

For the sauce

1 Pour a glug of red wine into a saucepan, bring to the boil, then add the stock. Return to the boil and reduce for around 15 minutes until thickened. Stir in the conserve and simmer until glossy.
2 Add the fresh blackberries and rabbit legs to the sauce, including any juices that have collected. Set aside.

To serve

1 Season the rabbit loins with salt and pepper. Heat two tablespoons of olive oil, and a knob of butter in a frying pan until foaming. Add the loins and cook for one minute on each side, then remove from the pan.
2 Serve with roasted baby or chantenay carrots and a potato dish, such as dauphinoise. Arrange the vegetables on a plate, slice the rabbit and place around the vegetables, add a glazed leg to each plate, and pour over the blackberry sauce.

Top Tip: Take care not to overcook the meat as it will become very dry.

"Never panic about trying new flavours: it can only go one of two ways!"

Lee Groves

Lee Groves, Head Chef, The Turks Head, Penzance

"Cooking, whether at home or in a professional kitchen, is like approaching a dog: if you're scared of it, it will bite you! Never panic about trying new flavours: it can only go one of two ways!

One of my favourite ingredients is pak choi, it's so versatile: cooked, raw in salads, steamed and stir fried, it works well with both meat and fish, and is also a good vegetarian choice. And now it's grown in Cornwall!

Being proud of what you do, having a happy team, and especially having happy customers is more than any individual proud moment. Lack of communication in the kitchen is the most dangerous part of the job: no-one wants to get burnt by someone else! So, if you are right behind me, and I have a hot pan, and you don't tell me you are there...

On my first night of working in a restaurant – world class at the time – I was asked to strain the stock pots and put all the bones in the bin. The following morning at 7am the head chef asked me: 'Where is the oxtail?'... Oops!"

Phil Boddington, Owner, Boddington's Berries, Mevagissey

"We grow strawberries and make preserves on the farm, for the discerning customer. Our fruit is supplied locally to shops, wholesalers and catering establishments, and our preserves travel the country to independent retailers, caterers and bakers. I always encourage people to buy British when they're sourcing ingredients.

I'm very proud to still be growing strawberries after many difficult years supplying the supermarkets. It's especially exciting to find ourselves exporting to Japan and Australia.

When I need to unwind from work, I find that Guinness usually does the trick!"

Spice-crusted Cornish Duck duck breast with creamy polenta, confit sauce, Savoy cabbage and butternut squash balls

Recipe by Matthew Dale, Head Chef, The Boskerris Hotel, St Ives

For the duck
½ tsp cardamom seeds
½ tsp cumin seeds
½ tsp juniper berries
½ tsp Madras curry powder
2 duck breasts, 350g each, fat side lightly scored with crosses
Sea salt and ground pepper

For the polenta
500ml chicken stock
80g instant polenta
80ml double cream
50g Gruyère cheese, grated
2 tbsp unsalted butter

For the confit plum sauce
1 tbsp duck fat, melted
3 shallots, chopped
200ml port
600ml veal stock

For the vegetables
½ savoy cabbage
½ butternut squash
4 cloves garlic
1 tbsp butter
Small handful pistachio nuts

To cook the duck
1 In a small, dry, heavy-based pan, toast the cardamom, cumin and juniper over a medium heat for two or three minutes, shaking occasionally, until fragrant. Transfer to a spice mill or pestle and mortar and cool before grinding to a powder. Transfer the spice mix to a small bowl and stir in the curry powder.
2 Season the duck breasts with sea salt and pepper then coat with the spice mix, rubbing it in. The duck breasts can be refrigerated overnight, or used immediately.
3 In a medium frying pan, cook the duck fat-side down over a medium-low heat for 15 to 20 minutes until the fat has rendered and the skin is richly browned. Turn the meat over and cook for three to five minutes until a thermometer inserted horizontally into the centre of the meat registers 50°C for rare and 55°C for medium rare. Transfer to a board and rest the meat for five minutes.

To make the confit plum sauce
Heat the duck fat in a pan over a medium heat. Meanwhile, fry the shallots for one to two minutes, until softened. Add the port, simmer until reduced in volume by half, then add the stock. Simmer until reduced to a syrupy consistency and thick enough to coat the back of a spoon. Set aside to cool.

To cook the polenta
In a medium saucepan, bring the stock to boiling. Gradually

Continued on page 135...

stir in the polenta and return to the boil. Cook over medium-low heat for about three minutes, stirring often, until thickened. Remove the pan from the heat and stir in the cream, cheese and butter. Season.

To cook the Savoy cabbage
Remove and discard the side leaves, then wash and thoroughly pat dry the remaining cabbage. Cut out and throw away the middle stem then slice the cabbage finely. Blanch in boiling water for three to four minutes, then drain and sauté in butter for two minutes. Season to taste.

To cook the butternut squash balls
Halve a butternut squash and scoop out the seeds. Rub the flesh with garlic and olive oil then put three cloves of garlic in the middle of the squash and season with Cornish sea salt and pepper. Turn upside down and roast for 45 minutes at 220°C/gas mark 7. Remove from the oven, cool for 10 minutes then scoop out balls with a melon baller.

To serve
Cut the duck breasts crosswise into 6mm slices. Spoon the polenta onto plates and top with the duck slices. Season with Cornish sea salt and serve with the confit sauce, cabbage and squash balls. The spicy juices from the burnished duck breast soak into the superbly rich polenta. Sprinkle pistachio crumbs over the dish just before serving.

> "This particular dish balances our lite bites menu in the autumn. The inspiration came from southern French cooking."
> Matthew Dale

Roger and Tanya Olver, Directors of The Cornish Duck Company Ltd, Truro

"We produce our own duck to supply to top restaurants in Devon and Cornwall, as well as direct to the general public. When sourcing ingredients, we'd encourage people to check the provenance of the produce, ensure it's locally reared, grown or caught and to go direct to the producer.

The best part of what we do is the feedback we get from customers. And even after ten years, hatching the ducklings is still amazing! Processing the ducks is the worst part – but it's necessary to ensure the best possible welfare for the birds as they don't have to travel.

We have our own cross of traditional breeds and are proud of the fact that we care for them from incubation to delivery (known as 'Hatch to Dispatch')."

Gluten-free Polgoon Sparkling Elderflower Wine and raspberry sponge

Recipe by Nicola Osborne, Proprietor, Trengwainton Tea Rooms, Madron, Penzance

For the sponge

50g soft butter
150g soft margarine
200g caster sugar
4 medium eggs
225g gluten-free self-raising flour
2 tsp gluten-free baking powder
2 tbsp Polgoon Sparkling Elderflower Wine

For the filling

250g mascarpone cheese
250ml double cream
50g icing sugar
2 tbsp Polgoon Sparkling Elderflower Wine
200g fresh raspberries

For the coulis

100g fresh raspberries
½ tbsp water
½ tbsp caster sugar

Icing sugar to dust the cake

Top Tip: Most supermarkets now stock gluten-free flour and gluten-free baking powder.

To make the sponge

1 Preheat the oven to 170°C/gas mark 3 and line two eight-inch cake tins by greasing with butter, dusting with flour and inserting a disc of baking parchment onto each bottom.
2 Put all ingredients into a bowl, sieve the flour and baking powder and gently mix with an electric mixer until combined. Turn the mixer to full power and beat for one to two minutes.
3 Divide the cake mixture evenly between the tins. Gently level the mixture with a round-bladed knife.
4 Place in the middle of the oven and bake for approximately 25 minutes. When the sponges are ready they'll be golden and spring back when gently pressed.
5 Remove the cakes from the oven and carefully turn out onto cooling racks. Peel off the baking parchment and turn them up the right way. Leave to cool.

To make the filling

Place all the ingredients, except the raspberries, into a bowl and gently mix until thick enough to hold its shape. Cover and refrigerate until required.

To make the coulis

Combine all ingredients in a small bowl and microwave until the water bubbles. Stir and sieve the mixture into a small jug.

Continued on page 141...

To assemble the cake

1 Once the sponges are cool, turn upside down and spread with the mascarpone cream filling.
2 Wipe over the raspberries with a paper towel then arrange them on top. Drizzle over some of the raspberry coulis.
3 Place the other sponge on top and dust with icing sugar.

Nicola Osborne, Proprietor, Trengwainton Tea Rooms, Madron, Penzance

"Since starting at Trengwainton over nine years ago people have changed their diets, either through health reasons or personal choice.

This recipe shows that gluten-free food has come a long way in a short time. There is no need for sponges that look like a pancake and taste like cardboard.

Having travelled extensively, the whole ethos around food has always fascinated me and still does. I am lucky not to experience Monday morning blues but I think working in a walled garden with the occasional woodpecker flying by and working with like-minded people helps.

Cream teas are a speciality with us. So, when a friend rang and said she needed my scone recipe and a one-to-one lesson on making them as Prince Charles and Camilla were coming for a traditional Cornish Cream Tea, I naturally obliged. In fact they enjoyed them so much, Camilla returned and asked if they could take the rest back with them for the helicopter ride back home. Scones by Royal Appointment?"

"...a friend rang and said she needed my scone recipe and a one-to-one lesson on making them as Prince Charles and Camilla were coming for a traditional Cornish Cream Tea..."

"The best ingredients that you can source are the ones closest to you."

Kim Coulson, Owner and Partner,
Polgoon Vineyard and Orchard, Penzance

"Our vineyard and orchard in Cornwall grows and produces a range of award-winning wines and ciders as well as a range of artisan juices. We supply to some of the finest restaurants, farm shops, delis and bars around Cornwall and travel up to a few selected outlets in London, including Fortnum & Mason and the Flat Iron restaurants.

We have had a long-standing and excellent friendship with Trengwainton Tea Rooms, as we are next-door neighbours in Penzance. They have supported us as a local supplier for many years and we look forward to working together for many years to come. Trengwainton is a beautiful place and the food is exceptional, their focus on local provenance is at the forefront of the meals they produce, with many ingredients even grown on site. Nicola does a wonderful job and it's a real treat to take time out and have lunch there.

The best ingredients that you can source are the ones closest to you. We are very proud of the fact that we both grow and produce our wines and can call ourselves single estate.

There are lots of things that I love about my job: the fact that we work so closely with the local community, that we have developed a range of relationships, that we get to produce quality products in one of the most beautiful parts of the world. Though the worst part of running a small family business is that sometimes there isn't enough time to make the most of such a beautiful place.

At the end of the busy week we head down as a family to our local pub on the seafront. When the summer kicks in I love taking my youngest girls to their surfing lesson at Sennen Beach on a Sunday morning.

The proudest moment for John, my husband, and I was tasting the grape juice for our very first wine in 2006. The most exciting thing was to then follow up by winning the Waitrose Trophy for Best Rosé in the UK. An incredible achievement with our first wine."

Wheal Charlotte Pizza, using Cornish Yarg

Recipe by Jon and Vicki Crwys-Williams,
The Cornish Pizza Company, St Agnes

Makes two thin-crust, 12-inch pizzas

For the dough base

250g plain flour
5g fresh or dried yeast
5g salt
5g olive oil
150g tepid water

For the tomato sauce

400g tin chopped tomatoes, or 6
    large, ripe tomatoes
1 tsp oregano, fresh or dried
1 tsp basil, fresh or dried
2 tsp tomato puree
Pinch of salt
Pinch of sugar
Pinch of ground black pepper

For the topping

120g Cornish Yarg, grated
24 capers
24 pitted black olives, halved
24 semi sun-dried tomatoes, halved
40g pine nuts
2 cloves of garlic, finely chopped
Handful of fresh basil leaves, torn into
    small pieces
Sea salt and pepper

Semolina flour to dust worktops

To make the pizza base

1 Place the dry ingredients into a bowl, making sure that the yeast is kept separate from the salt until the water is added, either by putting the salt and yeast in different sides of the bowl or by burying the yeast in the flour.
2 Add the oil and tepid water (ideally 19°C-24°C) and mix to form a soft dough. Turn out the dough and knead for about 10 to 12 minutes until it's smooth and elastic.
3 Weigh out the mixture into two 250g dough balls. Cover and leave to prove for at least an hour and a half.
4 Once proved, refridgerate the dough until you are ready to use it (within 72 hours).

To complete the pizza

1 Blend all the tomato sauce ingredients to a smooth consistency in a food mixer on high speed. Season.
2 Put a baking tray or pizza stone into the oven and preheat to 220°C/gas mark 7.
3 Dust the worktop lightly with flour then gently knead the dough. Allow it to rest for 15 minutes – it will be easier to work with at room temperature – before rolling out to form a 12-inch/30-cm round.
4 Lightly dust the preheated baking tray then place the pizzas onto it. Working quickly, top the pizzas with a generous layer of tomato sauce, spreading it to the edges. Arrange the toppings evenly. Lightly season.
5 Bake for eight to ten minutes, until crisp and golden then remove from the oven.
6 Sprinkle over the torn fresh basil and serve immediately.

"Cornish Yarg can be a great alternative to traditional Italian mozzarella. The edible nettle rind gives a delicate mushroom flavour."

Jon Crwys-Williams

Jon and Vicki Crwys-Williams, The Cornish Pizza Company, St Agnes

"We started our company in 2012 and we make fresh, authentic thin-crust pizza using local ingredients. A Cornish twist is evident in everything we do, from using local suppliers to having Cornish mine names for our pizzas.

The Wheal Charlotte pizza is our take on a deconstructed pesto sauce using pine nuts, capers, tomatoes, garlic and torn basil. Topping it with Cornish Yarg gives it a zingy alternative to traditional mozzarella.

We have used Cornish Yarg on our pizzas since we started. Delicious, it adds a 'gooeyness' to a pizza. We love the little speckles of green nettle when it has been grated.

Pizza is deceptively simple – a freshly made dough base, stretched as thinly as you can, a selection of fresh local toppings, a quick bake and there you have it. If only it were that easy! With few ingredients there is nowhere to hide and the quality of the base is critical."

Scallops served with Boscastle Farm Shop Hogs' Pudding

Recipe by Will Sherry, Head Chef, Boscastle Farm Shop

Ingredients

12 to 16 scallops

350g hogs' pudding

200ml white-wine vinegar

125g caster sugar

2 tsp arrowroot, mixed with a few
   drops of water

100g pea shoots

50g red amaranth (a bright purple
   micro salad with an earthy flavour)

To make the dressing

1 Put the vinegar and sugar into a pan and boil until the sugar dissolves.
2 Stir the arrowroot and water into this mixture and allow to cool.

To cook the scallops

1 Heat a little sunflower oil in a pan and sear the scallops for one minute on each side, making sure not to overcook.
2 Cook the hogs' pudding for a similar amount of time until it's golden on both sides.

To serve

1 Arrange the pea shoots and red amaranth on plates and lightly drizzle with dressing. Use the remaining dressing to glaze the scallops.
2 Serve with artisan bread for a tasty weekend lunch or as a simple starter.

Top Tip: Cooking should be fun, keep things simple, seasonal, local... and calm!

"It's fantastic to be able to create genuinely local, seasonal dishes."

Will Sherry, Head Chef, Boscastle Farm Shop

"We have our own traditional butchery here, together with a sea view! It's fantastic to be able to create genuinely local, seasonal dishes.

We regularly hold signature evenings in the restaurant, showcasing produce made on the farm. This scallop dish has consistently been a firm favourite starter. As a chef, I am so lucky to be able to meet with the farmer and butcher daily, plus also having a fishing boat just half a mile away.

The best bit of my job is working with passionate, like-minded foodies. I'm proud to be Head Chef in such a dynamic and vibrant, award-winning place.

I unwind from my day by cycling 10 miles home from the coast to the moor."

Thank you to the following Taste of the West award-winners who made this recipe book possible

The Artisan Kitchen
07779 998129
theartisankitchen.co.uk

Ashburton Delicatessen
01364 652277
ashburtondelicatessen.co.uk

Bell & Loxton
01548 562023
bellandloxton.co.uk

Boddington Berries
01726 842346
boddingtonsberries.co.uk

Boscastle Farm Shop & Café
01840 250827
boscastlefarmshop.co.uk

Boskerris Hotel
01736 795295
boskerrishotel.co.uk

The Cornish Duck Co.
01726 882383
cornishduck.com

The Cornish Pizza Company
01872 553092
thecornishpizzacompany.co.uk

Chesil Smokery
01308 456306
chesilsmokery.com

Clavelshay Barn
01278 662629
clavelshaybarn.co.uk

Duchy of Cornwall Nursery Café
01208 872668
duchyofcornwallnursery.co.uk

Dukes
01395 513320
dukessidmouth.co.uk

Favis of Salcombe
01548 521182
favis-os.com

Kittow's Butchers
01726 814926
kittowsbutchers.co.uk

The Lordleaze Hotel
01460 61066
lordleazehotel.com

Martin's Meats
01242 621493
martinsmeats.com

Moreton Tearooms
01929 463647
moretontearooms.co.uk

Orange Elephant Ice Cream
01392 833776
tavernersfarm.co.uk

Otterton Mill Café
01395 567041
ottertonmill.com

Otter Vale Products
01884 35000
ottervaleproducts.co.uk

Polgoon Vineyard & Orchard
01736 333946
polgoon.com

Rebecca's Kitchen
07749 054915
rebeccaskitchen.co.uk

River Exe Café
07761 116103
riverexecafe.com

Rock Salt Cafe & Brasserie
01752 225522
rocksaltcafe.co.uk

The Samphire Bush
01752 253247
thesamphirebush.co.uk

The Scarlet Hotel
01637 861800
scarlethotel.co.uk

Sharpham Wine and Cheese
01803 732203
sharpham.com

Sladers Yard
01308 459511
sladersyard.wordpress.com

Trengwainton Tearooms
01736 331717
trengwaintontearooms.com

Tudor Farmhouse Hotel
01594 833046
tudorfarmhousehotel.co.uk

Two Bridges Hotel
01822 892300
twobridges.co.uk

The Watercress Company
01929 463241
thewatercresscompany.co.uk

Worth Matravers Tea & Supper Room
01929 439368
worthmatraverstearoom.co.uk

The Anchor Inn
01297 489215
theanchorinnseatown.co.uk

Blackdown Eggs
01460 234883
blackdownhillseggs.co.uk

Godminster
01749 813733
godminster.com

Hinton Harvest
07939 485260
hintonharvest.co.uk

Lynher Dairies Cheese Company
01872 870789
lynherdairies.co.uk

Palmers Brewery
01308 422396
palmersbrewery.com

Quicke's
01392 851222
quickes.co.uk

South Devon Chilli Farm
01548 550782
southdevonchillifarm.co.uk

The Turks Head Inn
01736 363093
turksheadpenzance.co.uk

Apple

Scallops with Kittows Hogs' Pudding 118

Twice-baked Cornish Yarg soufflé 122

Arborio risotto rice

Sharpham Cremet and Jerusalem artichoke risotto 90

Artichoke

Mediterranean Sharpham Ticklemore Goat cheese slice 72

Asparagus

Martin's Meats Longhorn beef sirloin, mushroom ketchup, wild garlic and asparagus 20

Golden-fried hen's egg, chive hollandaise and asparagus on a potato cake, using Blackdown Hills West Country Eggs 30

Smoked salmon, asparagus and Godminster Brie with Cracked Black Pepper tart 44

Favis of Salcombe crab benedict with blanched asparagus 82

Aubergine

Mediterranean Sharpham Ticklemore Goat cheese slice 72

Baby leaf salad

Sea bass with sizzled ginger, chilli and spring onions, served with Watercress Company Baby Leaf Salad 66

Baby spinach

Martin's Meats Longhorn beef sirloin, mushroom ketchup, wild garlic and asparagus 20

Banana

Orange Elephant Banoffee baked alaska 112

Banoffee ice cream

Orange Elephant Banoffee baked alaska 112

Basil

Wheal Charlotte Pizza, using Cornish Yarg 144

Bay leaf

Roasted breast of Hinton Harvest Sasso chicken, braised leg ravioli, crispy wing, spring vegetables and tarragon 38

Favis of Salcombe crab benedict with blanched asparagus 82

Roasted breast of duck, charred chicory with fig and date jus, using Otter Vale jelly and relish 96

Beef

Martin's Meats Longhorn beef sirloin, mushroom ketchup, wild garlic and asparagus 20

Blackberries

Chesil Smokery smoked duck salad with blackberry ketchup 62

Roast Cornish rabbit with Boddington's Berries Blackberry Conserve and fresh blackberries 128

Black truffle

Sharpham Cremet and Jerusalem artichoke risotto 90

Brown shrimp

Coronation brown shrimp with spiced pineapple chutney, using Otter Vale Coronation Sauce 94

Butternut squash

Spice-crusted Cornish Duck Company duck breast with polenta, confit sauce, Savoy cabbage and squash balls, 132

Cabbage

Spice-crusted Cornish Duck Company duck breast with polenta, confit sauce, Savoy cabbage and squash balls, 132

Capers

Wheal Charlotte Pizza, using Cornish Yarg 144

Carrots

Roasted breast of Hinton Harvest Sasso chicken, braised leg ravioli, crispy wing, spring vegetables and tarragon 38

Roasted breast of duck, charred chicory with fig
and date jus, using Otter Vale jelly and relish 96

Celery
Roasted breast of Hinton Harvest Sasso chicken,
braised leg ravioli, crispy wing, spring
vegetables and tarragon 38
Roasted breast of duck, charred chicory with fig
and date jus, using Otter Vale jelly and relish 96

CHEESE
Cheddar
Dorset Lobster mac and cheese with Palmers
Best Bitter sauce 56
Smoked ham hock & Quicke's Mature
Cheddar terrine with Jail Ale pickled onion,
cheese toasty and cheese beignet 106

Cornish Yarg
Twice-baked Cornish Yarg soufflé 122
Wheal Charlotte Pizza, using Cornish Yarg 144

Dorset Blue Vinny
Dorset Lobster mac and cheese with Palmers
Best Bitter sauce 56

Godminster Brie with Cracked Black Pepper
Smoked salmon, asparagus and Godminster
Brie with Cracked Black Pepper tart 44
Chorizo, wild garlic and Godminster Brie with
Cracked Black Pepper croquettes and
lemon aioli 46

Gruyère
Spice-crusted Cornish Duck Company duck
breast with polenta, confit sauce, Savoy
cabbage and squash balls, 132

Mascarpone
Gluten-free Polgoon Sparkling Elderflower
Wine and raspberry sponge 138

Parmesan
Cremet and Jerusalem artichoke risotto 90

Sharpham Cremet
Sharpham Cremet and Jerusalem artichoke
risotto 90

Ticklemore Goat
Mediterranean Sharpham Ticklemore Goat
cheese slice 72

Chicken (Sasso)
Roasted breast of Hinton Harvest Sasso chicken,
braised leg ravioli, crispy wing, spring
vegetables and tarragon 38

Chicken stock
Roasted breast of duck, charred chicory with fig
and date jus, using Otter Vale jelly and relish 96
Spice-crusted Cornish duck breast with creamy
polenta, confit sauce, Savoy cabbage and
butternut squash balls 132

Chicory
Roasted breast of duck, charred chicory with fig
and date jus, using Otter Vale jelly and relish 96

Chilli
Sea bass with sizzled ginger, chilli and spring
onions, served with Watercress Company
Baby Leaf Salad 66
Coronation brown shrimp with spiced pineapple
chutney, using Otter Vale Coronation Sauce 94
Dressed native blue lobster cocktail using Bell &
Loxton Rapeseed Oil for the mayonnaise, with
fennel, apple & chilli 100

Chives
Golden-fried hen's egg, chive hollandaise and
asparagus on a potato cake, using Blackdown
Hills West Country Eggs 30
Mediterranean Sharpham Ticklemore Goat
cheese slice 72
Gazpacho soup with Favis of Salcombe crab 76
Coronation brown shrimp with spiced pineapple
chutney, using Otter Vale Coronation Sauce, 94

Chocolate
South Devon Chilli Farm chocolate fondant 86

Chorizo
Chorizo, wild garlic and Godminster Brie with Cracked Black Pepper croquettes and lemon aioli 46

Coriander
Gazpacho soup with Favis of Salcombe crab 76
Dressed native blue lobster cocktail using Bell & Loxton Rapeseed Oil for the mayonnaise, with fennel, apple & chilli 100

Coronation sauce
Coronation brown shrimp with spiced pineapple chutney, using Otter Vale Coronation Sauce 94

Courgette
Chesil Smokery smoked duck salad with blackberry ketchup 62

Crab
Gazpacho soup with Favis of Salcombe crab 76
Favis of Salcombe crab benedict with blanched asparagus 82

CREAM
Double cream
Martin's Meats Longhorn beef sirloin, mushroom ketchup, wild garlic and asparagus 20
The Artisan Kitchen's Blaisdon Red Plum Jam soufflé with plum ripple ice cream 24
Smoked salmon, asparagus and Godminster Brie with Cracked Black Pepper tart 44
Dorset Lobster mac and cheese with Palmers Best Bitter sauce 56
Orange Elephant Banoffee baked alaska 112
Spice-crusted Cornish Duck Company duck breast with polenta, confit sauce, Savoy cabbage and squash balls, 132
Gluten-free Polgoon Sparkling Elderflower Wine and raspberry sponge 138

Single cream
Twice-baked Cornish Yarg soufflé 122

Crème fraîche
Lemon pots with raspberry sauce and meringue, using Rebecca's Kitchen Lemon Curd 52

Cucumber
Gazpacho soup with Favis of Salcombe crab 76
Scallops with Kittows Hogs' Pudding 118

Dill
Scallops with Kittows Hogs' Pudding 118

Duck
Chesil Smokery smoked duck salad with blackberry ketchup 62
Roasted breast of duck, charred chicory with fig and date jus, using Otter Vale jelly and relish 96
Spice-crusted Cornish Duck Company duck breast with polenta, confit sauce, Savoy cabbage and squash balls, 132

Elderflower wine
Gluten-free Polgoon Sparkling Elderflower Wine and raspberry sponge 138

Fennel bulb
Dressed native blue lobster cocktail using Bell & Loxton Rapeseed Oil for the mayonnaise, with fennel, apple & chilli 100

Fig
Roasted breast of duck, charred chicory with fig and date jus, using Otter Vale jelly and relish 96

Garlic
Martin's Meats Longhorn beef sirloin, mushroom ketchup, wild garlic and asparagus 20
Golden-fried hen's egg, chive hollandaise and asparagus on a potato cake, using Blackdown Hills West Country Eggs 30
Chorizo, wild garlic and Godminster Brie with Cracked Black Pepper croquettes and lemon aioli 46

Sea bass with sizzled ginger, chilli and spring
   onions, served with Watercress Company
   Baby Leaf Salad 66
Gazpacho soup with Favis of Salcombe crab 76
Roasted breast of duck, charred chicory with fig
   and date jus, using Otter Vale jelly and relish 96
Scallops with Kittows Hogs' Pudding 118
Wheal Charlotte Pizza, using Cornish Yarg 144
Spice-crusted Cornish Duck Company duck
   breast with polenta, confit sauce, Savoy
   cabbage and squash balls, 132

Ginger
Sea bass with sizzled ginger, chilli and spring
   onions, served with Watercress Company
   Baby Leaf Salad 66
Coronation brown shrimp with spiced pineapple
   chutney, using Otter Vale Coronation Sauce 94

Gluten-free baking powder
Gluten-free Polgoon Sparkling Elderflower Wine
   and raspberry sponge 138

Gluten-free self-raising flour
Gluten-free Polgoon Sparkling Elderflower Wine
   and raspberry sponge 138

Greek-style yoghurt
Lemon pots with raspberry sauce and meringue,
   using Rebecca's Kitchen Lemon Curd 52

Green pepper
Gazpacho soup with Favis of Salcombe crab 76

Ham hock
Smoked ham hock & Quicke's Mature Cheddar
   terrine with Jail Ale pickled onion, cheese
   toasty and cheese beignet 106

Hazelnut
Martin's Meats Longhorn beef sirloin, mushroom
   ketchup, wild garlic and asparagus 20
Dorset Lobster mac and cheese with Palmers
   Best Bitter sauce 56

Hogs pudding
Scallops with Kittows Hogs' Pudding 118
Scallops served with Boscastle Farm Shop Hogs'
   Pudding 148

Jerusalem artichoke
Sharpham Cremet and Jerusalem artichoke
   risotto 90

Juniper berry
Chesil Smokery smoked duck salad with
   blackberry ketchup 62

Kohlrabi
Martin's Meats Longhorn beef sirloin, mushroom
   ketchup, wild garlic and asparagus 20

Leek
Roasted breast of duck, charred chicory with fig
   and date jus, using Otter Vale jelly and relish 96

Lemon
Scallops with Kittows Hogs' Pudding 118

Lemon curd
Lemon pots with raspberry sauce and meringue,
   using Rebecca's Kitchen Lemon Curd 52

Lobster
Dressed native blue lobster cocktail using Bell &
   Loxton Rapeseed Oil for the mayonnaise, with
   fennel, apple & chilli 100
Dorset Lobster mac and cheese with Palmers
   Best Bitter sauce 56

Macaroni
Dorset Lobster mac and cheese with Palmers
   Best Bitter sauce 56

Madras curry powder
Spice-crusted Cornish Duck Company duck
   breast with polenta, confit sauce, Savoy
   cabbage and squash balls, 132

Micro herbs
Gazpacho soup with Favis of Salcombe crab 76

Mixed leaves
Chesil Smokery smoked duck salad with
   blackberry ketchup 62

MUSHROOMS
Chestnut
Martin's Meats Longhorn beef sirloin, mushroom
   ketchup, wild garlic and asparagus 20

Girolle
Martin's Meats Longhorn beef sirloin,
   mushroom ketchup, wild garlic and
   asparagus 20

Shittake
Smoked ham hock & Quicke's Mature
   Cheddar terrine with Jail Ale pickled onion,
   cheese toasty and cheese beignet 106

Nasturtium leaves
Martin's Meats Longhorn beef sirloin, mushroom
   ketchup, wild garlic and asparagus 20

Olives
Mediterranean Sharpham Ticklemore Goat
   cheese slice 72
Wheal Charlotte Pizza, using Cornish Yarg 144

Onion
Roasted breast of Hinton Harvest Sasso chicken,
   braised leg ravioli, crispy wing, spring
   vegetables and tarragon 38
Gazpacho soup with Favis of Salcombe crab 76
Coronation brown shrimp with spiced pineapple
   chutney, using Otter Vale Coronation Sauce 94
Smoked ham hock & Quicke's Mature Cheddar
   terrine with Jail Ale pickled onion, cheese
   toasty and cheese beignet 106

Oregano
Wheal Charlotte Pizza, using Cornish Yarg 144

Panko breadcrumbs
Golden-fried hen's egg, chive hollandaise and
   asparagus on a potato cake, using Blackdown
   Hills West Country Eggs 30
Chorizo, wild garlic and Godminster Brie with
   Cracked Black Pepper croquettes and lemon
   aioli 46

Parsley
Roasted breast of Hinton Harvest Sasso chicken,
   braised leg ravioli, crispy wing, spring
   vegetables and tarragon 38
Mediterranean Sharpham Ticklemore Goat
   cheese slice 72
Dressed native blue lobster cocktail using Bell &
   Loxton Rapeseed Oil for the mayonnaise, with
   fennel, apple & chilli 100

Pea shoots
Scallops with Kittows Hogs' Pudding 118
Scallops served with Boscastle Farm Shop Hogs'
   Pudding 148

Pineapple
Coronation brown shrimp with spiced pineapple
   chutney, using Otter Vale Coronation Sauce 94

Pine nuts
Wheal Charlotte Pizza, using Cornish Yarg 144

Pistachio nuts
Orange Elephant Banoffee baked alaska 112
Spice-crusted Cornish Duck Company duck
   breast with polenta, confit sauce, Savoy
   cabbage and squash balls, 132

Plum jam
The Artisan Kitchen's Blaisdon Red Plum Jam
   soufflé with plum ripple ice cream 24

Polenta
Spice-crusted Cornish duck breast with creamy
   polenta, confit sauce, Savoy cabbage and
   butternut squash balls 132

Pork stock

Smoked ham hock & Quicke's Mature Cheddar terrine with Jail Ale pickled onion, cheese toasty and cheese beignet 106

Port

Roasted breast of duck, charred chicory with fig and date jus, using Otter Vale jelly and relish 96

Spice-crusted Cornish Duck Company duck breast with polenta, confit sauce, Savoy cabbage and squash balls, 132

Potato

Chorizo, wild garlic and Godminster Brie with Cracked Black Pepper croquettes and lemon aioli 46

Potato (mashed)

Golden-fried hen's egg, chive hollandaise and asparagus on a potato cake, using Blackdown Hills West Country Eggs 30

Puff pastry

Mediterranean Sharpham Ticklemore Goat cheese slice 72

Rabbit

Roast Cornish rabbit with Boddington's Berries Blackberry Conserve and fresh blackberries 128

Rapeseed oil

Dressed native blue lobster cocktail using Bell & Loxton Rapeseed Oil for the mayonnaise, with fennel, apple & chilli 100

Chesil Smokery smoked duck salad with blackberry ketchup 62

Raspberries

Gluten-free Polgoon Sparkling Elderflower Wine and raspberry sponge 138

Lemon pots with raspberry sauce and meringue, using Rebecca's Kitchen Lemon Curd 52

Real ale

Smoked ham hock & Quicke's Mature Cheddar terrine with Jail Ale pickled onion, cheese toasty and cheese beignet 106

Dorset Lobster mac and cheese with Palmers Best Bitter sauce 56

Red amaranth

Scallops served with Boscastle Farm Shop Hogs' Pudding 148

Red onion

Golden-fried hen's egg, chive hollandaise and asparagus on a potato cake, using Blackdown Hills West Country Eggs 30

Red pepper

Mediterranean Sharpham Ticklemore Goat cheese slice 72

Red wine

Roasted breast of duck, charred chicory with fig and date jus, using Otter Vale jelly and relish 96

Roast Cornish rabbit with Boddington's Berries Blackberry Conserve and fresh blackberries 128

Salad leaves

Twice-baked Cornish Yarg soufflé 122

Savoy cabbage

Spice-crusted Cornish Duck Company duck breast with polenta, confit sauce, Savoy cabbage and squash balls, 132

Scallops

Scallops with Kittows Hogs' Pudding 118

Scallops served with Boscastle Farm Shop Hogs' Pudding 148

Sea bass

Sea bass with sizzled ginger, chilli and spring onions, served with Watercress Company Baby Leaf Salad 66

Shallots

Chesil Smokery smoked duck salad with blackberry ketchup 62

Favis of Salcombe crab benedict with blanched asparagus 82

Sharpham Cremet and Jerusalem artichoke risotto 90

Roasted breast of duck, charred chicory with fig and date jus, using Otter Vale jelly and relish 96

Smoked salmon

Smoked salmon, asparagus and Godminster Brie with Cracked Black Pepper tart 44

Sosa airbag farina

Smoked ham hock & Quicke's Mature Cheddar terrine with Jail Ale pickled onion, cheese toasty and cheese beignet 106

Spring onion

Sea bass with sizzled ginger, chilli and spring onions, served with Watercress Company Baby Leaf Salad 66

Dressed native blue lobster cocktail using Bell & Loxton Rapeseed Oil for the mayonnaise, with fennel, apple & chilli 100

Smoked ham hock & Quicke's Mature Cheddar terrine with Jail Ale pickled onion, cheese toasty and cheese beignet 106

Tarragon

Roasted breast of Hinton Harvest Sasso chicken, braised leg ravioli, crispy wing, spring vegetables and tarragon 38

Favis of Salcombe crab benedict with blanched asparagus 82

Thyme

Martin's Meats Longhorn beef sirloin, mushroom ketchup, wild garlic and asparagus 20

Roasted breast of Hinton Harvest Sasso chicken, braised leg ravioli, crispy wing, spring vegetables and tarragon 38

Roasted breast of duck, charred chicory with fig

and date jus, using Otter Vale jelly and relish 96

TOMATO

Gazpacho soup with Favis of Salcombe crab 76

Wheal Charlotte Pizza, using Cornish Yarg 144

Cherry tomato

Gazpacho soup with Favis of Salcombe crab 76

Semi-dried sun blush tomato

Mediterranean Sharpham Ticklemore Goat cheese slice 72

Sun-dried tomato

Wheal Charlotte Pizza, using Cornish Yarg 144

Turnip

Martin's Meats Longhorn beef sirloin, mushroom ketchup, wild garlic and asparagus 20

Veal stock

Spice-crusted Cornish Duck Company duck breast with polenta, confit sauce, Savoy cabbage and squash balls, 132

Vanilla pods

The Artisan Kitchen's Blaisdon Red Plum Jam soufflé with plum ripple ice cream 24

Walnuts

Twice-baked Cornish Yarg soufflé 122

Walnut (candied)

Sharpham Cremet and Jerusalem artichoke risotto 90

Wild garlic

Chorizo, wild garlic and Godminster Brie with Cracked Black Pepper croquettes and lemon aioli 46

Smoked ham hock & Quicke's Mature Cheddar terrine with Jail Ale pickled onion, cheese toasty and cheese beignet 106